The 25 Best Reptile and Amphibian Pets

R. D. Bartlett

Full-color Photographs

BARRON'S

About the Author

R. D. Bartlett is a herpetologist who has authored more than 600 articles and numerous books on reptiles and amphibians. He lectures extensively and has participated in field studies across North and Latin America. In 1970, he began the Reptilian Breeding and Research Institute, a private facility. Since its inception, more than 200 species of reptiles and amphibians have been bred there, some for the first time in the United States under captive conditions.

Acknowledgments

For photographic opportunities, thanks are due to Chris McQuade (Gulf Coast Reptiles), Rob MacGinnis (Glades Herp), Bill Love (Blue Chameleon Ventures), Bill Brant (The Gourmet Rodent), Randy Limburg, Brian Emanuel, and Dan Scolaro. Additional thanks to Randy Limburg, Terry Dunham, and Bruce Miller (Redding Reptiles) for providing insight into the natural history of rosy boas and sand boas. And to David Rodman, my editor, my sincere appreciation for suggestions and patience in accomplishing the completion of this book.

© Copyright 2006 by Barron's Educational Series, Inc.

All inquiries should be addressed to:
Barron's Educational Series, Inc.
250 Wireless Boulevard
Hauppauge, New York 11788
www.barronseduc.com

Library of Congress Catalog Card No. 2005050021

ISBN-13: 978-0-7641-3251-3
ISBN-10: 0-7641-3251-2

Library of Congress Cataloging-in-Publication Data
Bartlett, Richard D., 1938–
 The 25 best reptile and amphibian pets / Richard D. Bartlett.
  p. cm.
 Includes index.
 ISBN 0-7641-3251-2
 1. Reptiles as pets. 2. Amphibians as pets. I. Title: Twenty-five best reptile and amphibian pets. II. Title.

SF459.R4B376 2006
639.3'9—dc22   2005050021

Printed in China
9 8 7 6 5 4 3 2

Photo Credits
R. D. Bartlett

Cover Photos
R. D. Bartlett

Important Note

This book tells the reader how to purchase and care for reptiles and amphibians. The author and publisher consider it important to point out that the advice given in this book is meant primarily for normally developed reptiles and amphibians of excellent physical health.

Anyone who purchases a reptile or amphibian should watch it carefully, especially its behavior toward humans. Caution is advised in the association of children and other pets with reptiles and amphibians. If you are scratched or bitten by a reptile or amphibian, you should consult a doctor as soon as possible.

Even carefully supervised reptiles and amphibians sometimes can damage to someone else's property or cause accidents. It is therefore in the owner's interest to be adequately insured against such eventualities, and we strongly urge all owners to purchase a liability policy that covers their pets.

Contents

Chapter One

Understanding Reptiles and Amphibians

Reptiles

Reptiles are so diverse that to use the blanket statement "understanding reptiles" is not only pretentious but it is an impossibility. After all, there are the snakes, amphisbaenids, and lizards (which together form one group), the turtles (chelonians), the crocodilians, and the rhyncocephalians (the tuataras). This assemblage of more than 6,500 species is so diverse that some herpetologists do not consider all to be reptiles.

It is within the snakes, amphisbaenids, and lizards that we find the greatest diversity in lifestyles. Among this group (the Squamata) are some that are aquatic, many that are terrestrial, a few that are fossorial, and still others that are arboreal. Within these subgroups we have the heliotherms (sun worshippers), those that burrow, and accomplished arborealists (tree dwellers). Turtles are traditionally divided into three groups; marine, semiaquatic, and terrestrial. In the United States the latter forms are referred to as tortoises. The croc-

odilians are semiaquatic and the rhyncocephalians (only two species) are rare terrestrial dwellers of islands off the coast of New Zealand.

If we continue to subdivide, we find that a few reptiles have extended their ranges northward into boreal climes, many more are adapted to temperate climates, and a host of species are of tropical distribution. Then, of course, it becomes

Few snakes are prettier than an Everglades rat snake, Elaphe obsolete rossalleni, *but some are inclined to bite when handled.*

An odd-colored California kingsnake.

necessary to differentiate the arid-land species from those of the rain forests and those of river- and lakeside habitats from the many that prefer open grasslands.

Many of the more common snakes, some lizards, and a few of the turtles and tortoises are now among the most popular reptile pets. Since most of the common forms of reptiles are habitat generalists, they are somewhat less demanding captives than the amphibians. Many species have lived for 20 or more years as captives.

Amphibians

Despite often being mentioned in the same breath (as in "Reptiles and Amphibians") amphibians are not closely allied to the reptiles at all. The regimen of care needed to maintain amphibians is very different from that provided for most reptiles.

There are three groups of amphibians: the anurans (frogs, toads, and treefrogs), the caudatans (salamanders, including newts), and the gymnophionans (the caecilians), which together number more than 4,000 species. Among all groups are species that are exclusively aquatic, many that are seasonally aquatic (surface water is sought for breeding activities), some that are terrestrial, inhabiting moist places, and a few that are desert dwellers (but that are still dependent on ground moisture to sustain life). Within the frogs and the salamanders are species that are arboreal, many that are terrestrial, a few that are aquatic, and some that burrow persistently. The caecilians (all of which are limbless) are divided into aquatic and terrestrial forms.

Note: Amphibians are even less tolerant of handling than reptiles. All species should be considered "just look, don't touch" pets. When it does become necessary to handle amphibians it is imperative that you wash your hands thoroughly before doing so. Topical hand creams, medications, or insecticides may cause the almost instantaneous death of your pet. Many very successful keepers and breeders of amphibians wear sterile, discardable plastic gloves when it is necessary to handle the creatures. Since amphibians produce toxins (irritants) in skin or parotoid (shoulder) glands, if you don't wear the gloves, wash your hands again *after* handling the amphibians.

Moisture Requirements

Because amphibians absorb most of their moisture requirements through permeable skin, it is necessary that they be kept on clean, moist substrate. Cleanliness is especially important, for as water is absorbed, so too can life-threatening impurities be absorbed.

Depending on the species of amphibian being maintained, moist sphagnum moss, forest soil, or even damp sand may be suitable substrates. Some hobbyists simplify things even more, providing only a layer or two of damp, unbleached paper towels as the substrate and a shallow dish of water in which the amphibian can soak if it desires. This can suffice for all but burrowing species, which should be provided with a clean, moist medium in which they can burrow.

Habitat

After choosing the substrate, the terrarium should be tailored toward

Theloderma corticale, *the Vietnam mossy treefrog, is a new and seemingly hardy addition to the American pet trade.*

the natural history of the amphibian. Treefrogs should be provided with branches of suitable diameter on which they can climb. Terrestrial species should be provided with hiding areas (rock caves or even plastic hideboxes will suffice). We place live

Eastern kingsnakes, Lampropeltis getula getula, *are quite large and may be snappy.*

Western banded geckos (the San Diego subspecies, Coleonyx variegatus abbotti, *is shown here) are small, hardy captives.*

terrarium plants such as "pothos" (*Epipremnum aureum*) in our terraria. Live plants provide not only additional visual barriers, but through transpiration assist in maintaining humidity in the terrarium.

Aquatic species such as underwater frogs and axolotls must be kept, like fish, in fully aquatic conditions.

Aeration and filtration (but not a strong current) are of benefit to aquatic amphibians.

Life Histories

Of the thousands of diverse reptile and amphibian species, only a comparative handful are maintained in captivity, and we still know only the

Not all house snakes are equally easy to keep. The beautiful aurora house snake, Lamprophis aurora, *is usually a delicate captive.*

Variable kingsnakes are just that— variable in both color and pattern.

HANDLING YOUR PET REPTILES AND AMPHIBIANS

Reptiles, to a species, do not like to be physically restrained, and many of them do not tolerate physical restraint, including casual handling, well—after all, in the wild, to be restrained is usually to be dominated, injured, or even eaten. Small wonder reptiles don't like to be restrained! For the most part reptiles should be considered "display pets" rather than "interactive pets." In other words, most reptiles are far more content in captivity if merely observed in their terrarium rather than when they are handled. In some cases, when a nervous reptile is restrained, it may become sufficiently upset to interrupt a normal feeding schedule or other daily activities.

Reptiles dislike being approached from above. In the reptile mind, such an approach probably equates to an attack by a predatory bird, or the pounce of a hunting bobcat or fox. When it is necessary to approach your reptile, if you do so from the side and grasp it gently but firmly to lift it, the creature will probably object less. Remember, too, that many reptiles (snakes especially) hunt by scent. If you have the smell of mice, or worms, or frogs on your hands, this may evoke a feeding response and even the tamest reptile may bite.

Wash and rinse your hands carefully or use sterile latex gloves to handle amphibians. Newts, axolotls, and underwater frogs should be handled in a small aquarium fishnet. When the net contains an animal, cover the top with your free hand to prevent escape.

For the safety of your pet, when handling any reptile it is important that your hands are clean and have no traces of topical insecticides, medications, or lotions. Many of these can be harmful to your reptile and some can be fatal.

However, with all of the above admonitions said, the reason we have chosen the 25 species of reptiles presented in this book is because they are not only hardy and easily cared for, but are for the most part, placid, among the more easily handled, and difficult to throw off a feeding routine. Of the 25, the rather nervous Honduran milksnake would be the most difficult to handle, and even it is not actually hard to do.

barest rudiments of the life histories of many of these.

The life histories of others, of course, especially of the common types (corn snakes, kingsnakes, leopard geckos, bearded dragons, and horned frogs among them), has been largely unraveled, but there are none, common or rare, about which we do not still have unanswered questions. Therefore, rather than trying to provide an inadequate overview of the life history of reptiles at the outset, there is a rather comprehensive account in each of the species accounts (beginning on page 33)—but there are a few overviews that can be provided.

Chapter Two

Caging

To decide what constitutes proper caging conditions for a captive herp, it is necessary that you understand the natural history of that species.

Enclosures

All reptiles should be provided ample room and escape-proof cages. Sand boas (collectively, snakes of well-drained aridlands) and the desert-dwelling bearded dragon should not be kept in a humid, closed terrarium with a large water bowl. Nor should a corn snake, a species of the humid southeastern forest and agricultural lands, be maintained in a desert terrarium. The time to learn what is needed is *before* you acquire the reptile, not after you have made an impulse purchase. No matter how common, how inexpensive they may be, every pet deserves the very best captive conditions that you are able to provide. The fact that proper enclosures for some animals are far more expensive than the animals themselves, becomes very apparent if you choose to keep such reptiles as anoles (not covered in this book) or some garter snakes. The reptiles may

cost only $5 or $10 but the setups may be triple that cost or more.

Reptiles and amphibians seem to instinctively find the weakest point in their caging, and will escape through seemingly impossible apertures. Cage all very securely. Locking plastic- or metal-framed screen covers for aquaria of various sizes are a standard stock item in most pet stores.

As mentioned earlier, husbandry specifics are dealt with in the individual species accounts. Choose your reptile pet wisely, taking into consideration the time you can allocate to its care, the space you have available, and, if your time is limited, the ambient conditions Mother Nature has given you to work with. It is always easier and quicker to work within the parameters naturally provided than to try to alter them—but the latter *can* be accomplished.

Besides being escape-proof, cages must be suitably large, have a heat source (if necessary), and lighting. Some states (Florida being one) have guidelines regarding the size and type of cage needed for many species of reptiles and amphibians.

Today, a vast array of commercial reptile cages is available to hobby-

A plant, a limb, a water dish, paper towel substrate, and a suitable aquarium can make a serviceable cage for many species of reptiles and amphibians.

ists. Unless you choose to do so, it is no longer necessary to convert aquaria into terraria, but there is certainly nothing wrong with doing so.

As long as they can be kept clean and adequately ventilated, a caging setup can be flamboyant, Spartan, or somewhere in between these two extremes.

Plastic shoe, sweater, and blanket boxes are often used and all are available in most hardware and department stores. Be sure the covers fit securely, or can be secured with tape or Velcro strips.

Plastic Caging

If plastic caging is used, sufficient air (ventilation) holes must be drilled (or melted) through the sides to provide adequate air transfer and to prevent a buildup of humidity. Venti-

lation should be provided on at least two sides and, if possible, on all four sides. If an aridland species is being kept, ventilate the top as well.

Cabinets that hold a dozen or more plastic boxes are now available, many with heat tapes built in. These are advertised in most reptile magazines and are available at many of the reptile meets. Keep in mind that many of these units are formidably expensive.

Cage Furniture

Security

To thrive as captives reptiles and amphibians must feel secure. The needed security may be provided by limbs, rocks, or other visual barriers, or by providing the creatures with

Vertical orientation, limbs, and a screen front are ideal for arboreal species, such as the tropical rat snake, Spilotes pullatus.

hideboxes or other easily sterilized cage ornamentation into, beneath, or behind which the animals may retreat when they choose. Live plants may be used to increase cage humidity, or, if higher humidity is undesirable, plastic vines may be used for benign ornamentation.

Cage decorations and visual barriers may be as simple as an inverted, disposable cardboard hidebox with an access hole cut in one side, or as complex as cemented-in-place tiered rocks against the back of the terrarium. Textured waterbowl-hide-box combinations are also readily available.

The Hide

Cage furniture should either be so light that if it shifts it cannot injure your pet, or, if heavy, should be adequately secured to prevent the herps from injuring themselves. Snakes seem most comfortable if their hide is so small that their coiled body presses against both the sides and the top. Whether the hide is a simple cut-to-size cardboard box or a commercial preformed plastic cave is immaterial. Hollow limbs (not cedar or other aromatic tree species) and cholla (cactus) skeletons are also commercially available.

Gently curved corkbark slabs and tightly curled corkbark tubes are commercially available, lightweight alternatives to hollow limbs and are easily cleaned and sterilized for lengthy use.

Note: Position the hides, whether cork, boxes, or cave, prudently.

Rocks

Rocks, by definition, are heavy (except for pumice, which we feel is too rough to be satisfactory) and, should they accidentally shift, may easily injure or kill your herp. Rocks must be held in place with latex aquarium sealant. If flat rocks are used as cage-bottom hides, spacers of smaller rocks should be cemented

in place to prevent the large ones from settling on and crushing your pets.

Substrate

Your cage-bottom substrate should be of a type that is easily cleaned or readily replaced. Substrates consisting of a thick layer of nonaromatic mulch (cypress or aspen are ideal; cedar or strongly aromatic pine, which contain phenols that are harmful to herps, are not), or fallen leaves, are excellent. Several layers of paper towels or newspaper are equally good for many species. Smooth-grained sand or loam may be ideal for some species, but inappropriate for others.

An ornate horned frog peeks out from his burrow in sphagnum moss substrate.

Cleanliness

Cages (including substrate and furniture) should be regularly cleaned and sterilized. There are excellent cleansing products available in most pet stores that are nontoxic to reptiles and amphibians. A dilute solution of Clorox bleach can also be safely used. Cages must be thoroughly rinsed after sterilization.

Do not clean cages with any solution containing pine oils or other aromatic additives—contact with, or breathing the fumes of, these, even after the cage has been carefully rinsed, may be toxic to the snakes.

Lighting and Heating

The ability to thermoregulate is important for captive herps. Being ectotherms, these creatures are dependent on their keepers to provide them with caging that permits

them to select their optimum body temperature. Warming the cage can be accomplished with under-cage heating pads and heating tapes, or with hot rocks (because of the possibility of burns the latter are not particularly recommended), or with above-cage lighting.

Provide thermal gradients except during hibernation, when the terrarium temperature should be uniformly cool. Normal night temperatures can be cooler by several degrees than daytime temperatures. In small tanks, we put the hidebox on the cool end of the tank; if the tank is sufficiently large, we put a hidebox on both ends.

Full-spectrum Lighting and Natural Sunlight

Four important components in the diet of your herps are calcium, phosphorus, vitamin D_3 (this can be in the form of beta-carotene), and the ultraviolet rays UV-A and UV-B.

• UV-A induces normal activity patterns in herps, while UV-B apparently helps lizards synthesize vitamin D_3. When D_3 is not adequately present, calcium depletion can result, even when calcium is sufficient.

• The ratio of phosphorus to calcium is also important. At least twice as much calcium as phosphorus should be given.

• Although natural sunlight is the best supplier of UV-A and UV-B, some of the better full-spectrum bulbs now on the market can produce enough to make a difference in the health of your pet herp. These bulbs are expensive, but well worthwhile.

• To best avail the herps of natural sunlight, they can be placed in a wood and wire cage in an open screened window (both window glass and cage glass filter out the beneficial UV rays and will allow a potentially lethal heat buildup) or, when and where possible, moved outdoors in a cage of wood and wire construction.

• Calcium and D_3 additives may also be used to augment the diets of your herps.

It seems that additives and full-spectrum lighting are more important to diurnal insectivores and herbivores than to nocturnal species or those that consume whole endothermic prey.

Chapter Three

Feeding and Watering Techniques

It is not enough to simply feed your reptiles and amphibians—you must feed them correctly. The food must be appropriate for the herp species in question and must contain the proper nutrients, including vitamin D_3 and calcium. If you are feeding an insectivorous species, it is not enough that the insects be alive—they must be alive and healthy.

Both food and water must be placed where your reptile or amphibian will recognize it and use it readily. It must also be presented in a manner that will not cause your pet to ingest substrate or other foreign matter when drinking or eating.

Acclimating your pet to accept a food item that it would not naturally accept, or presenting a diet of a single prey item, may not be in the best long-term interests of your herp. Thoroughly research the dietary needs of your pet.

The Basics

Menu Notes

Do not feed herbivorous or omnivorous lizards or turtles spinach or any other vegetable containing oxalic acid or other oxylates. In reptiles, oxylates prevent proper calcium utilization.

A tropical rat snake eats a prekilled mouse.

Garter snakes thrive on a diet of nightcrawlers.

Prekilled rodents are strongly recommended for those species that eat them. Live rodents can cause injury to a reptile predator. Although snakes such as rosy boas, corn snakes, and house snakes are capable of great jaw distention, it is still better to offer two or three smaller mice than one gigantic one. The larger the meal, the more apt it is to

Unlike many worms, nightcrawlers cannot live in tainted soil. These large worms are an ideal herp food.

be regurgitated if the snake becomes frightened or temperature-stressed. The jaws of sand boas and king-snakes are less distensible. Smaller prey is definitely better for these species.

Food Insect Care

A poorly fed or otherwise unhealthy insect offers little but chitinous bulk when fed to a reptile or amphibian. To maintain your insectivorous herps in good health, they must be fed healthy insects. The term "gut-loading" is used for insects fed healthy food just before they, themselves become a meal for your lizard, salamander, or frog. Foods such as grated apples, carrots, broccoli, squash, fresh alfalfa and/or bean sprouts, honey, vitamin/mineral-enhanced (chick) laying mash, or commercial cricket diet, are only a few of the foods that may be provided for your crickets and giant mealworms. Regular mealworms enjoy a diet of fresh bran or other cereal with a little apple or potato for moisture. Most insects eat rather continuously and will lose much of their food value if not fed for just a few hours.

Vitamin/Mineral Supplements

There are many dietary vitamin/ mineral supplements that can be used to stabilize or augment a herp's calcium intake.

The vitamin/mineral supplements that we have used over the years are as follows:

• OSTEO-FORM (Calcium and phosphorus with vitamins), a product of Vet-A-Mix, Inc. of Shenandoah, Iowa, contains an excellent ratio of calcium to phosphorus. It has about twice as much of the former as the latter as well as vitamin A, vitamin D_3, and vitamin C.

• REP-CAL is 100 percent calcium and entirely devoid of phosphorus. It is a product of Rep-Cal Research Labs of Los Gatos, California. It also contains vitamin D_3.

• Miner-all, is available in two formulas, one with vitamin D_3 for indoor use and one without vitamin D_3 for outside use. It is produced by Sticky Tongue Farms in Sun City, California.

• Avitron is a liquid bird vitamin. It is ideal for mixing with the fruit formula relished by crested geckos and blue-tongued skinks. It is a product of Lambert Kay and is available in many pet shops worldwide.

Gray crickets should be gut loaded before being fed to your pets.

How much should you offer and how frequently? For adults, add a pinch of the powder over their food (this includes dusting the insects) twice weekly. For younger, smaller, rapidly growing herps or for adult females that are in any stage of egg formation or deposition, add a small pinch of the powdered vitamin daily.

Herps with unlimited access to natural, unfiltered sunlight will require less vitamin D_3 supplementation than lizards having little or no access.

Watering

Fresh water must be presented in a way that is recognizable and usable by the reptile or amphibian you are keeping. The water should be kept clean and fresh at all times. How it is presented will depend on

Mid-Baja rosy boas, Charina trivirgata saslowi, *are small and beautiful.*

what species of reptile or amphibian you are keeping. All of the snakes, the tortoise, and most of the lizards will readily drink water from a low bowl. If the bowl is large enough, many of these creatures will occasionally soak in it as well. This is especially true if cage humidity is a little low or if the herp is entering its shedding cycle.

Randy Limburg was the first to develop a line of red-eyed albino rosy boas.

Although amphibians are very different from reptiles and require a rather moist cage or terrarium, most species will also utilize a water bowl for soaking. However, for the most part, amphibians absorb their water requirements from their moist terrarium surroundings. For this reason the terrarium home of an amphibian should be misted frequently. The terrarium should be moist, but not wet. Again, the water must be chlorine/chloramine-free and kept clean.

Reptiles and amphibians often stool in their water bowl, necessitating immediate cleaning and sterilizing.

Aquatic amphibians, of course, absorb their moisture requirements from the water in which they live. Again, cleanliness is imperative.

Cage Humidity

Besides serving as a drinking receptacle, the water bowl can play an integral part in raising or lowering the humidity in a cage. Cage humidity will be higher in a cage with littler ventilation than in one with a good air flow.

If you wish to increase, then retain, a high humidity in your cage, place a large water bowl in the hottest spot (over a heating pad if one is in use). If you wish to decrease, or keep humidity as low as possible, provide a small water dish and place it in the coolest spot in the cage.

The Hydration Chamber

The use of a hydration chamber can do much to revitalize moisture-deprived, dehydrated amphibians and reptiles.

A hydration chamber can be constructed of wire mesh over a wood frame, or of an aquarium equipped with a circulating water pump and a screen or perforated Plexiglas top. If you are fortunate enough to live in a benign climate where the cage can be placed outdoors, a mist nozzle can be placed on the end of a hose, affixed over the cage, and fresh water of moderate temperature run through this for an hour or more a day.

Warning: If your community chlorinates or chloramines the water supply, the "mist nozzle" technique can be detrimental to amphibians, all of which have permeable skins.

If indoors, the cage can be placed on top, or inside, of a properly drained utility tub and the freshwater

With growth, the pattern on this coastal rosy boa (from near Barrett Lake, California) will fade.

system used. Again, chlorinated or chloramined water can be harmful to amphibians. Adjust water temperature carefully. It is imperative that the drain system be adequate and kept free of debris if this system is used indoors. A secondary (backup) drain (just in case) might do much to guarantee your peace of mind.

In contained systems, the circulation pump can force water from the tank itself through a small-diameter PVC pipe into which a series of lateral holes have been drilled, or merely brought up to the top of the tank and allowed to drip through the screen or perforated Plexiglas. It is imperative that the water in self-contained systems be kept immaculately clean.

Chapter Four

Choosing Your Reptile or Amphibian Pet

Beautiful and exotic reptiles and amphibians of many species and of varying suitability as pet species can be found in myriad venues. But considerations greater than whether a reptile or amphibian is pretty, affordable, or interesting must be weighed when you are considering a purchase. Among these other considerations are issues such as whether the creature is healthy and the ease with which it can be kept. In other words, can you house and feed it properly?

Captive Bred Versus Wild Collected

Captive-produced reptiles and amphibians are often less stressed, hardier, and easier to acclimate to new conditions than wild-collected examples of the same species. Captive-bred herps are also usually easier to cycle for breeding, and are less likely to harbor untenable numbers of internal parasites.

However, I am not certain of the validity of the frequently heard argu-

ment that captive breeding reduces collecting pressures on wild populations. This may be true in the future, but I have seen very few hobbyists, either established or budding, bypass a wild specimen that they can collect legally. Nevertheless, we unequivocally advocate the acquisition of captive-bred herps over those collected from the wild.

Where to Find Pets

Reptile and amphibian pets of numerous species can be found in venues as commonplace and traditional as pet shops or, if legal, collecting them from the wild. Two relatively new sources of reptile and amphibian pets are herp expos and the Internet.

Herp Expos

"Herp expos" have now become mainstream. It seems that there are one or more expos at some point in America and Europe almost every weekend. At these shows you not only have an opportunity to pick and

Many species of European newts are beautiful, but all, such as this Spanish marbled newt, Triturus marmoratus, *require cool water temperatures.*

choose the species in which you are interested, but you will be able to meet other interested and experienced keepers.

In addition to the more common species, relative rarities are occasionally found at these shows and because of the great competition among dealers, prices are usually very fair. Locations and dates of herp expos can be found on reptile hobbyist Web sites and in reptile magazines.

Internet and Classified Ads

Today, many reptile dealers and breeders offer their products via the cyber world. By instructing your search engine to look for "reptile dealers" or a specific species, you can often locate many species of reptiles and amphibians for sale (see Web addresses on pages 151–152). Classified ads in reptile magazines are also a good source for these snakes.

Buyers beware! As with any other mail order transaction, you should know your dealer or their reputation.

Making the Choice

Simply stated, the care that is suitable for one species of reptile or amphibian would not necessarily be the best for another. Prior to acquisition, it is important to research the appearance and habits of the reptile or amphibian in which you are interested. Know what the creature should look like. Is it a slender and active or a corpulent and sedentary species? Is it diurnal or nocturnal? What is its natural diet and can you easily duplicate the food items necessary? Look at live examples in zoos, nature centers, in the wild, or at pictures in books or on the Internet.

Once you have decided on a herp pet, if possible, inspect the actual animal you intend to acquire for physical anomalies:
• malnourishment, scars; abnormal scales
• encrustations near the mouth or nostrils
• retained sheds

The gray treefrog is intricately patterned, may be gray or green, and is as easily kept as a green treefrog.

The Chaco horned frog, Ceratophrys cranwelli, is as easily kept as the ornate horned frog and is available in albino specimens.

The tropical African fire skink, Riopa fernandi, is more colorful, smaller, requires less room, and is nearly as easily kept as the Australian blue-tongued skink.

• clear eyes, free of any cloudiness or opacities (unless it is a snake and in shed)
• swelling.

Also look for the following:

• Snakes sometimes fail to shed the brille (the modified scale that covers the eye), which can eventually lead to eye infections.
• Look for edges of dry skin around the edges of the eye or an eye that looks "filmy."
• Look at the belly to ascertain that there are no burns (such as from a malfunctioning hot rock), open sores, or blisters.
• Amphibians should have no vestiges of red coloration (except for species in which this is a normal coloration) on the belly. The ventral scutes (snakes) or scales (lizards) should not have yellowish or brownish edges.
• When snakes and lizards become malnourished they develop longitudinal folds of loose skin along the sides or the outlines of their ribs. Ill or malnourished animals should be avoided.

These horned frogs are about to be shipped to a new owner.

• Ascertain that the reptile or amphibian is feeding properly and, if possible, actually observe it eating. A feeding herp is usually a healthy herp.

• Snakes and lizards may twitch or rub the face and body against cage furniture if they have mites. Mites are vectors of disease and need immediate eradication.

• Any reptile that is breathing with open mouth or has bubbles near the glottis or nostrils (amphibians do not manifest these symptoms) probably has a respiratory ailment. Reptiles that are suffering from respiratory infections may raise the forepart of their body and head off the ground and remain in this position for prolonged periods of time.

• Ascertain your potential herp's ability to crawl normally.

Avoid any reptiles or amphibians that demonstrate any of the above symptoms!

Shipping

Door-to-door deliveries of reptiles and amphibians, as well as airport-to-airport services are available. Shipping is not inexpensive, but it is fast and usually very reliable. It is best to not ship herps during very hot or very cold weather, or during high-travel holiday seasons. Unless you know your dealer well, it will usually be necessary to pay for

The European Hermann's tortoise, Testudo hermanni, *is hardy but may be difficult to acquire.*

the herp (and if prepaying is necessary, its shipping) in advance. Many dealers insist on cashier's checks, money orders, credit cards, or payment by Pay Pal. Do not hesitate to ask your dealer the method of payment required, as well as about what means or company the animal will be shipped by, which level of service will be used, estimated cost (including packing and handling), and the dealer's stance on DOA (dead on arrival) animals, in case an unfortunate accident does occur. Many dealers will guarantee live arrival if you work within their guidelines.

The Veterinarian

You may feel more secure if you have your veterinarian examine the animal before purchasing it, or at least immediately after acquiring the animal. This can be especially pertinent if the creature has been collected from the wild. Your veterinarian will be able to better assess

critical issues, such as appropriate hydration and weight, presence of internal parasites (almost ubiquitous with wild-collected herps), or diseases of the mouth or eyes. If problems are present, your veterinarian will be able to initiate a proper treatment regimen (see also the chapter on health, pages 25–31).

Favorite Pets

There are, in fact, many additional species of reptiles and amphibians (some closely allied to those discussed in this book) that make fine pets. Such longtime favorites as baby red-eared sliders and map turtles were omitted because of the difficulty keepers would have providing adequate facilities for the 10-inch-long (25-cm) adults. The beautiful yellow rat snake was omitted because it tends to be a bit larger than the related corn snake and may be just a bit more "snappy" as well. The California kingsnake and Honduran milksnake were chosen, not because they had any truly obvious advantages over other kingsnakes and milksnakes, but because they are the most readily available in the pet trade. Although the African spurred tortoise is more readily available than the red-footed tortoise, the former can attain immense sizes (more than 100 pounds [45 kg] in some cases, and if kept outside it has a tendency to dig large and very deep burrows). The Chaco horned frog is every bit as easily kept as the ornate horned frog, but the former is less variably colored.

As you can see, the choice was arbitrary. And the care of a larval tiger salamander, often referred to as a waterdog, is identical to that of an axolotl, but the former is not easily bred in captivity and is subject to drowning as it metamorphoses from its aquatic larval stage to the terrestrial adult stage. Again, the choice was arbitrary.

To offer you alternatives, pictures of some additional herps that make fine pets have been included here. The captions will refer you to the discussed species with the closest care regimen. The choice is yours. Enjoy!

Chapter Five

Breeding Captive Reptiles and Amphibians

Cycling

Although some reptiles in tropical regions are able to reproduce all year, the reproductive abilities of most are cyclically stimulated by climatic changes. Reptiles in temperate areas often breed following winter's hibernation (brumation), but some breed in the fall as they gather at

A hatchling amelanistic (albino) corn snake greets the world.

den sites. Other species may be induced to breed by the advent of the rainy season or by passing frontal systems that lower barometric pressure. Strangely, captive-bred reptiles seem to be less influenced by climatic stimuli than those in the wild. Some reptile species attain sexual maturity within the first year of life while others may not first breed until they are several years old. Some reptiles breed annually (egg layers may even multiclutch), some breed biennially, and some may breed even less frequently.

Eggs

A clutch may contain only one or two neonates or eggs (some geckos and skinks) to 100 or more (marine turtles and water snakes). The eggs require rather exact incubation parameters. Females of live-bearing species seek quite specific temperatures while gestating. Hatchlings or neonates are very like the adults of their species in form, but may vary dramatically in color. Eggs may be either hard-shelled (many turtles and tortoises) or soft-shelled (many lizards and snakes). Varying by species, the incubation duration may be as little as two weeks or as great as a year. The developing embryos of some reptile species undergo a diapause (a temporary cessation of development).

Babies

Baby reptiles are more apt to assume defensive or escape stances than the adults are. This is probably due to the fact that the babies are more vulnerable to predation than the adults. Baby turtles are very wary and will swim away at the slightest disturbance—not that adults are much less wary! Baby lizards are usually equally evasive, and baby snakes are quite apt to assume a striking pose and bite (this includes such normally benign species as the corn snake). But because they *are* babies, attitude should not preclude them being carefully handled when necessary or desired.

Incubating Reptile and Amphibian Eggs

Reptile eggs require some degree of heat to incubate successfully, while amphibian eggs are more adapted to relatively cool and changing temperatures.

Reptile eggs may be successfully incubated in moistened vermiculite, moistened perlite, or moistened

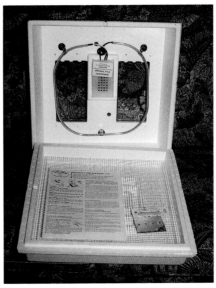

An example of an inexpensive incubator.

sphagnum. Some breeders prefer a mixture of the incubating mediums.

The soft-shelled eggs of turtles, lizards, and snakes can desiccate rapidly. It is important to monitor their progress, adding a bit of water to the substrate if the eggs show any indication of losing turgidity (turgidity is lost naturally a few days prior to hatching). The hard-shelled eggs of tortoises are more resistant to dehydration. However, it is equally important that the eggs, whether hard-shelled or soft-shelled, not be overhydrated. An inexact but simple way of determining the proper moisture content of the incubation medium is to thoroughly moisten it, then squeeze it as dry as possible in your tightened fists. The eggs should be placed directly on the substrate in a shallow depression to prevent

Eggs should be placed on a barely moistened substrate, then covered to maintain a high relative humidity.

them from accidentally turning. The exposed top of the eggs can be covered with a paper towel.

Important: Plan to have food of the proper kind and size on hand when the hatchlings emerge.

Companies such as Hovabator now produce inexpensive reptile-egg incubators. Be certain that you get one designed for reptile egg incubation. Some models intended for chick-egg incubation have a solid-state heating unit that is preset (and unadjustable) at a temperature too warm for the successful incubation of reptile eggs.

1. Carefully wash your hands before handling the eggs. Try to keep the eggs in the position in which they were lying.

2. Check the incubator temperature frequently and add a little water to the incubating medium as needed. The preferred humidity is 80 to 90 percent. A saturated atmosphere, where the moisture condenses and drips onto the eggs is not desirable. The medium of vermiculite or perlite should be kept damp to the touch but too dry to squeeze out any water with your hand.

3. Do not wet the eggs when you are remoistening the medium.

Collapsing: Both infertile and desiccating soft-shelled eggs will collapse during incubation. Hard-shelled eggs will not collapse but may crack. Infertile eggs usually develop a yellowish slimy-appearing shell. Discard these. For any number of reasons, embryo death may occur during incubation, or even as the full-term young are trying to break from their eggs.

Length of time: Varying by species and temperature, incubation may take between 65 to 88 days (rarely more than 200 days).

Hatching: After pipping, the babies may remain in the egg for several hours, or may emerge almost immediately. Once they have hatched they should be moved to another terrarium. Offer food and water after about 48 hours. The hatchlings should have their postnatal shed in several hours to a few days.

Chapter Six

The Health of Your Herps

Before acquiring any reptile or amphibian, find a veterinarian who is familiar with, has the ability to, and is willing to treat these creatures. Believe us when we say that not every veterinarian is qualified or willing. This is especially true of amphibian medicine. A veterinarian in your area can be found by instructing your computer's search engine to find the web site of the Association of Reptile and Amphibian Veterinarians.

Health Basics

As always, the starting point for assuring the good health of your herps begins with the basics. Start with healthy examples. Purchase your herp from a reliable supplier, but only after asking many pertinent questions, such as whether it is captive bred or wild collected, if it is feeding well, and if so, on what, and whether a fecal exam has been performed. If you are planning an on-line, mail-order purchase it is not always possible to actually see the reptile or amphibian in which you are interested, but the dealer/breeder can often post a high-resolution picture (jpg or tiff) of the actual creature. Although it is better to purchase a captive-bred or -born herp than a wild-collected one, this is not always possible.

Once ascertaining as fully as possible that the reptile or amphibian in question is in good health and actually the one you wish to acquire, assess your facilities (see Chapter Two).

• The cage you are providing must be both escape-proof and suitable in every aspect to the well-being of the inhabitant.

• The cage must provide sufficient space, adequate humidity (or lack of same), and a suitable temperature regime.

• You must be able to provide a supply of fresh water and suitable food.

• Proper cage temperature and relative humidity are very important factors.

• All facets of proper caging for the species involved must be addressed.

However, even with the best of care, health problems and concerns may occur. If caught in time, some health problems respond well to treatment, but others are irreversible, eventually fatal, and may be extremely communicable to other reptiles or amphibians. With the admonition once more that prevention is invariably better than cure, we will make mention of some possible health problems here.

Parasites

External Parasites

Ticks and mites are external parasites that can plague reptiles. Both are bothersome but rather easily combated. Ticks are usually present only on imported snakes but snake mites may be present on both imported and captive-born snakes. The latter are very easily transported from vendor to vendor and cage to cage. Both of these parasites have been implicated in the transmission of very serious, often fatal diseases, such as inclusion body disease. Eradicating them quickly is mandatory. Various methods of ridding your snakes of these pests exist. The methods vary from utilizing airborne insecticides such as "No-pest strips" (today's formula does not seem to be as reliable as the original) to desiccating the pests with Sevin or DryDie (desiccants are best used in low-humidity situations), to spraying the snake and its enclosure with dilute Ivermectin (this will be fatal to amphibians). Several commercially prepared mite eradication products are now available. We have had no practical experience with any of these.

Ivermectin: Ivermectin is easily administered from a spray bottle through any terrarium ventilation port and does not require that the boa be restrained. Administer the spray sparingly near the snake's head. Once the snake has been treated,

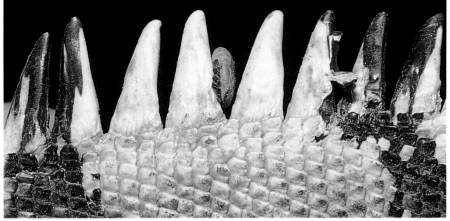

Ticks (one is between the dorsal spines on this spiny-tailed iguana), often found on wild-collected reptiles, should be promptly removed.

clean the cage, and any cage furniture, thoroughly and often. Wash all nooks and crannies and cage furnishings with a dilute Ivermectin solution or dilute bleach solution. Rinse the cage and furnishing thoroughly before reintroducing the snake to the cage. Be sure to wash and disinfect the holding cage in which the snake was placed while its permanent cage was being cleaned.

Since most treatments destroy only the mites themselves (leaving their eggs still viable), it will be necessary to treat the snakes at least twice (perhaps even three times) at nine-day intervals to kill hatching mites. If infested with mites, your snake will often rub its face and body along a shelf or perch, twitch, or soak incessantly in its waterbowl. Do not overlook these pests.

A regenerated tail (such as on this turnip-tailed gecko) is often of different shape and always of different scalation.

Internal Parasites

Endoparasites: Endoparasites, such as cestodes and/or protozoa, may be present. All are easily eradicated, but all do not respond to the same treatment. We suggest that you consult your veterinarian if treatment becomes necessary. Administering medications orally will require physically restraining the snake.

Cryptosporidium ssp. are almost omnipresent, but seldom cause distress to healthy reptiles. However, if snakes, or more rarely, lizards, are stressed or their immune system becomes suppressed, cryptosporidia may proliferate and quickly debilitate the reptile further. A proliferation of cryptosporidia will cause chronic, and often fatal, inability to digest food fully. If your reptiles begin to regurgitate frequently, seek veterinary assessment.

Injuries

Trauma (Burns, Bites, and Other Injuries)

Burns: The problem of thermal burns from a malfunctioning hot rock or improperly baffled bulb or ceramic heater is one that should never occur. Prevention is the best treatment. The primitive nervous system of reptiles and amphibians may allow these creatures to rest against a nonshielded light bulb or an overheating hot rock, even while burning themselves severely. Carefully shield all exposed light bulbs or ceramic heating units with a wire net or cage (taking care that there are no sharp edges on which the cage inhabitant can injure itself). Rather than hot rocks, use thermostatically controlled under-terrarium heaters to elevate cage temperatures for reptiles. Most amphibians are content at any moderate room temperature and may not require the use of an external heat source. Should a reptile sustain a burn, the injury should be dressed with an antibacterial burn ointment.

Because of their permeable skin that allows the absorption of topical medications, treating trauma on amphibians can be more difficult. Seek veterinary assessment.

Bites: Despite the fact that most snakes and carnivorous lizards will readily accept prekilled mice, many keepers choose to feed their reptiles live mice or rats. A bite by an adult rodent can be very serious. Although it is true that snakes and many lizards are predators that usually successfully overcome their prey with no incident, this is not always the case. Prey animals have been known to seriously injure reptiles in whose cages they have been left. Reptiles will often not make any effort to overcome an aggressive prey animal. The reptile may even refuse that particular kind of prey in the future. If bitten by a rodent in the eye, blindness may result. Mouthrot (infectious stomatitis) may develop from a bite or a scratch to the gums or mouth interior. Gaping wounds have been chewed into the sides of a reptile by an unmonitored rodent. We urge that all prey animals be prekilled or, if for some reason they are not, that they are never left unwatched in your reptile's cage. If your reptile is seriously bitten, a dressing of the wound with antibacterial powder may be necessary. Immediately seek veterinary assessment.

Other Injuries

Broken limbs or spinal injuries: These may occasionally occur if your herp pet sustains a fall while being carried or from an elevated position such as a basking site that is several feet above the floor. Broken bones are especially apt to happen if there has been an imbalance of calcium in the diet. Most broken limbs can be set successfully by your veterinarian. Spinal injuries are more serious and each must be individually assessed. Some may necessitate that the pet be euthanized. Support your herp while it is being carried, and if a favored elevated basking site is used, place a pillow beneath it.

Salamander appendage loss: This may occur during feeding frenzies, which is especially true of axolotls and the aquatic larvae of other mole salamanders and newts. Distressing though this may be to the keeper, legs, feet, gill stalks, and tail tips will be regenerated by these creatures. Appendage loss is less apt to occur in uncrowded aquaria having ample visual barriers such as plants, driftwood, or large smooth rocks. If appendage loss occurs, treat the water with a water conditioner such as Stresscoat, Novaqua, or Amquel.

Autotomized tail by lizards: This is a natural predator deterrent or

Besides being discomforting, mites (an adult mite is present on the snout of this Bolivian boa) are vectors of disease.

escape mechanism. Some lizard species even have fracture planes in the more distal caudal vertebrae (tail bones) to allow easy breakage if the tail is grasped by a predator (or keeper) but even if no fracture planes are present the tail may break. A degree of tail regeneration is normal for those species having fracture planes. A lesser degree of regrowth may occur when the tail is broken on species lacking fracture planes. If the tail is broken close to the body in the fleshy area, cauterization by a veterinarian may be necessary to staunch bleeding. The solution to this problem is normally simple: Do not grasp your lizard by its tail for any reason.

A cracked or broken shell on your turtle or tortoise can be caused by an accident (such as a drop). A veterinarian may be able to fiberglass (or otherwise patch) the break, allowing it to heal almost normally.

Mouth rot (infectious stomatitis): This can occur if a reptile's teeth or jaw are broken or its mouth lining is injured (by a rodent bite or other trauma such as striking at the side of its cage). The medication of choice can be Neosporin or a liquid sulfa drug. We have found both sulfamethazine and sulfathiazole sodium to be effective. If advanced to the stage where the snake's jawbones are affected and its teeth are loosened, veterinary assistance should be sought. This is a disfiguring disease that can be fatal if not treated. Acclimate your pet reptile to eating prekilled rodents, house it correctly, and do not withdraw sharply (breaking teeth) if you happen to be bitten.

Respiratory Ailments

These may plague a reptile maintained improperly or otherwise stressed. Respiratory distress is especially apt to occur when the cage humidity is high, the cage is damp, and temperatures are suboptimal. Not all cases respond to the same antibiotic; sensitivity tests must be made. Untreated respiratory ailments can become quickly debilitating and, if unchecked, eventually fatal. Seek veterinary assessment and help.

Bacterial, Fungal, and Viral Diseases

Vesicular dermatitis (blister disease syndrome): This may occur if a reptile is maintained in a damp and/or unclean cage. The causative agents for this disease can be many and the malady, which can ultimately be fatal, can be difficult to cure if in its advanced stages.

• Prolonged soaking in the water bowl may cause blistering. If a reptile persists in soaking, first check the animals for the presence of mites (treat immediately if found), then replace the bowl with a smaller one.

• Keep cage temperatures optimal.

• Prevent excessive humidity by providing adequate air flow and cage ventilation.

• Keep substrate dry and clean.

• Should vesicular dermatitis occur, immediately assess and correct your regimen of husbandry and seek the help of a reptile-oriented veterinarian.

• If the serum-containing blisters are numerous or if skin damage is apparent, lesions may already be present on internal organs. Sensitivity tests are necessary, and antibiotic treatment will necessarily be lengthy.

Redleg syndrome: This is a septicemic disease of amphibians kept in unclean or otherwise suboptimal caging, including overheated facilities, or in aquarium water having an excess of dissolved ammonia or bacteria. It is visible ventrally as a network of cutaneous hemorrhages (redness) and, if advanced, by a sloughing of the skin. If of bacterial origin it is communicable between amphibians and can be fatal. Quarantining each affected animal in a clean facility is a start. Although typically attributed to *Aeromonas* sp., other causative agents such as *Chlamydia* and *Basidiobolus* may be involved. Culturing, then specific treatment, should be performed by your veterinarian.

Edema syndrome: This syndrome is another bacterial malady of amphibians. Culturing, then specific treatment, is required, but even then, since kidney and liver dysfunction may occur, the disease is often fatal.

Paramyxovirus: This is a very communicable, insidious, and eventually fatal viral disease of some snake species. As it advances it causes spasms, loss of neuromotor control (especially noticeable in uncoordinated head motions), gaping, wheezing, and bloody mucus in the mouth. It has no known cure. This disease is highly contagious. The snake should be humanely euthanized. Know your supplier and quarantine all incoming snakes. Consult your veterinarian immediately.

Popeye: Popeye occurs in snakes when the space between the eye and the brille may become filled with discolored serum. This may be due to infection (often *Pseudomonas*) or injury of the eye or related ducts, or other causes. Blindness or loss of the eye may result. Consult a veterinarian promptly.

Improper shedding of the skin: This can lead to serious health issues. Improper shedding (retained eyecaps, etc.) may occasionally occur if your snake is not properly hydrated or if the cage humidity is too low. As your snake prepares to shed, a slightly higher cage humidity may resolve potential problems. Check the shed skin to ascertain that the eyecaps and tail tip have been shed. If it becomes necessary to physically assist in the shedding process, dampen the unshed skin slightly to render it pliable, and always remove the skin head to tail.

Nutritional Disorders

Corneal lipidosis (corneal opacity): This disorder has been seen in many amphibians, but its exact cause remains conjectural. The malady seems unknown in the wild, but is often seen in captive amphibians (White's treefrogs and various horned frogs among them) that are fed a uniform high-fat diet, whether of insects or rodents. Relative inactivity and advancing age can also be contributing causes. The cornea becomes partially or wholly opaque, causing blindness. A varied and, if possible, natural diet will probably avoid this problem.

Scoliosis (spinal curvature or irregularity): These problems are caused by an inadequate amount of vitamins in the diet or by the inability of the reptile or amphibian to utilize dietary vitamins and/or calcium that are present. It is often seen in neonate blue-tongued skinks, occasionally in bearded dragons, and often in amphibian tadpoles.

Vitamin D_3 and calcium additives have alleviated the problem in lizards; tadpoles provided with vitamin B complex additives have not developed the spinal deformities.

Pet Profiles

Corn Snake
Pantherophis guttata guttata

Description

Although it now seems from another lifetime, once, when a corn snake (also called **red rat snake**) was discussed, a beautiful gray to orange creature with red highlights came immediately to mind. There were no amelanistics (albinos), anerythristics (lacking red), or snow (lacking black and red pigments) corn snakes known. Aztec, butter, and milksnake corn snakes hadn't even been perceived—there were just plain old corn snakes.

Occasionally, an early breeder might designate an origin, such as Miami corn snake, or Okeetee corn snake, or maybe even New Jersey corn snake, but even that didn't matter much, because in the days of which I am speaking (the 1950s to the early 1970s), very little was known about genetics, and line-breeding for particular characteristics was not practiced. In fact, in those early days, almost all of the corn snakes in captivity were collected from the wild. But that changed in the 1970s when albino corn snakes were incorporated into breeding colonies. Following this,

Corn snakes are now bred in so many designer colors that some are difficult to identify.

wild populations of anerythristic corn snakes were found in southern Florida. Suddenly, corn snake keepers became geneticists and line-breeding for specific colors became the name of the game.

Today (2006) there simply is no way to adequately describe the colors and patterns that can be expected in a captive-bred corn snake. There are (conservatively) more than 30 designer colors and patterns of corn snakes available to hobbyists, and most are no more expensive than the original "wild" colorations. To make matters even more confusing, the genetics of many corn snakes are now so skewed that the breeding of two similar appearing examples may produce babies entirely unlike the parents in appearance.

Corn snakes, like all of the American rat snakes, are powerful constrictors. Adults readily accept prekilled mice as prey. The prey animals may be freshly killed or frozen, then thoroughly thawed. Almost all captive-bred hatchlings will eat pinky mice. But to ascertain that a hatchling is feeding properly it is always a good idea to check with the breeder/dealer or, better yet, to actually see the little snake eat.

A beautiful Okeetee-phase corn snake.

Size and Lifespan

Over a period of years, some corn snakes may attain an impressive size. The record size for a wild example is a rather heavy-bodied (but supple) 6 feet (1.8 m). However, most adults are fully mature at 30 to 54 inches (76–137 cm) in length with 48 inches (122 cm) being the average. Hatchlings vary between 8 and 12½ inches (20–31 cm) in length and are usually somewhat less colorful than the adults. If properly cared for, many captive corn snakes live for more than 10 years, and a few have lived for 20 or more years. As you can see, owning a corn snake can be a long-term investment of time.

Natural Range

The corn snake is a species of open mixed woodland, pinelands, barnyards, and the edges of agricul-

tural fields. It adapts well to disturbed habitats and can still be found in vacant lots and near the unkempt edges of warehouses in areas as populous as downtown Miami, Florida. It can be quite abundant where adequate cover (construction debris, discarded trash, abandoned or seldom-used buildings) exists. Although released or escaped specimens can now be found far from the described range of the corn snake, this serpent naturally ranges southward from the Pine Barrens of New Jersey, through Florida, including the Keys, and westward to Tennessee and Louisiana. The Great Plains rat snake, *Elaphe guttata emoryi*, continues the range well to northern Mexico, eastern New Mexico, and eastern Utah.

Captive Care

The corn snake is an excellent beginner's snake. One or two adults may be housed in a 20-gallon (76-L) long terrarium (12 × 12 × 30 inches [30 × 30 × 76 cm]). From one to several hatchlings may be maintained in a 5- to 10-gallon (19–38-L) capacity terrarium. If maintained communally, it is best that the snakes be fed separately or monitored very closely while eating. As with all rat snakes, fresh water must always be available. Many kinds of substrate are suitable—aspen shavings, pine shavings, newspaper, and dried leaves being just four of the choices. Because these snakes are adept at escaping, the terrarium must be covered with a lid (preferably of wire mesh) that can be clipped in place. A hidebox for the snakes should be considered essential. They prefer the smallest hidebox that they can hide in comfortably, so what is suitable for a hatchling or two will not suffice for an adult. Corn snakes will often rest comfortably on diagonally oriented or horizontal limbs of suitable diameter or on an elevated shelf. Corn snakes are quite temperature tolerant, but it is always best to provide a thermal gradient—88°F (31°C) on the warm end of the cage and room temperature (70–76°F [21–24°C]) on the cool end. This will allow your snake to choose the temperature at which it is most comfortable. You will probably notice that your corn snake will choose warmer temperatures when digesting a meal than when just resting quietly. Corn snakes will often utilize the warmth given off by an overhead light, especially to thermoregulate on a morning following a cool night.

Although the corn snake is able to climb, and may at times be found high in trees, it is less apt to do so than the related black, yellow, and gray rat snakes.

Breeding

It is very likely that when prey is normally plentiful and the snakes are able to maintain a good body weight, wild corn snakes breed annually; however, it is thought that wild corn snakes probably have only a single clutch of eggs each season. When well cared for in captivity, this snake species, in all of its many morphs, not only breeds each season, but often has two or even three clutches. If a third clutch is produced, it is often smaller than the earlier clutches and may contain a greater proportion of infertile eggs. Females differ from males in having a more slender and shorter tail. The tail of the male is heavy near the cloaca and long. Sexes are easily determined by probing.

Other Snakes with Similar Needs

Many species and subspecies of American, Eurasian, and Asian rat snakes will thrive when provided the conditions given the corn snake. Many of these rat snakes are larger when adult than the corn snake and will require a larger cage. Some are also quite apt to bite when surprised, a factor that should be considered when choosing your snake pet.

This is a Miami-phase corn snake.

California Kingsnake

Lampropeltis getula californiae

Description

This beautiful, hardy, and supple snake is the westernmost of the eastern kingsnake group. Not without good reason, this powerful constrictor is probably the most popular of the seven subspecies with hobbyists. The California kingsnake has now been captive bred for hundreds of generations and is available in many colors and patterns relatively inexpensively. The normal color of the California kingsnake is black or deep brown with either numerous broad cream to white bands or a white vertebral stripe. An example that was partly banded and partly striped was rarely found. Today, to these natural colors, albinos, lavenders, and banana yellows have been added and the patterns have been either reduced or enhanced as well. California kingsnakes that are 50 percent yellow and 50 percent brown are now commonplace, as are those once rare partially striped, partially banded examples. This snake has a narrow head, but is rather heavy bodied when adult. It is immune or at least resistant to the effects of bites from venomous snakes.

A high-yellow California kingsnake.

Size and Lifespan

This is one of the smaller of the kingsnakes. Most are adult at a length of 3.5 feet (1.1 m). Occasional examples may attain 4.5 feet (1.4 m) in length. A lifespan of 15 (or more) years may be expected from California kingsnakes.

Range

The California kingsnake is widely distributed in the western United States and the Baja Peninsula. It ranges southward from southwestern Oregon to Cabo San Lucas and eastward to eastern Arizona and southwestern Colorado. It occurs from low to moderate elevations in sparsely vegetated deserts and on hillsides well wooded with pines. It is often associated with rocky regions, trash heaps, and riparian habitats. In other words the California kingsnake is a habitat generalist. Favored hiding sites are beneath trash at the edges of irrigation canals. Escaped or unwanted and released pet California kingsnakes are now being found as far east as Florida.

Captive Care

Kingsnakes are noted for the broad range of prey that they nor-

A banded albino California kingsnake.

mally accept. Insects, amphibians, other reptiles, including lizards, baby turtles, and venomous and harmless snakes, and small birds and small mammals are all avidly eaten. Captives feed well on small prekilled rodents.

Cleanliness is mandatory when housing kingsnakes—any snakes for that matter—but *especially* kingsnakes. If maintained in suboptimal conditions (such as on a damp, or *especially* a damp and unclean, substrate), kingsnakes are very prone to developing the difficult to cure (and potentially fatal) blister disease syndrome (see page 30). However, if their quarters are clean and dry, these are among the hardiest of snakes. A thermal gradient of from 87°F (30.5°C) on the warm end to 70 to 80°F (21–26.5°C) on the cool end of the terrarium should be provided.

A single adult California kingsnake can be maintained in a 20-gallon (75.7-L) long terrarium (12 × 12 × 30 inches [30 × 30 × 76 cm]). A pair should have a 40-gallon (151-L) "breeder" tank (these vary in size by manufacturer, but are usually in the 18 × 16 × 36-inch [46 × 40 × 91-cm] range). Babies can be maintained in much smaller terraria, but remember, kingsnakes are prone to cannibalism and many babies seem particularly so. It is usually better to keep the babies separately.

Kingsnakes are secretive and will burrow readily if able. They seldom voluntarily climb. One or more hideboxes and visual barriers such as limbs or rocks on the floor of the cage will help provide a feeling of security. A dish of clean drinking water is mandatory but if your snake routinely uses it for long soaks,

A normal banded California kingsnake.

reduce the size of the dish to prevent the snake from doing so. When startled, California kingsnakes may "S" their neck and strike if approached. Some have the disconcerting habit of pressing their nose against the side of your hand or a finger, then methodically biting and chewing. Handle them carefully and remain alert.

Breeding

Kingsnakes collected from the wild may require an 8- to 12-week period of hibernation to cycle reproductively. Captive-bred and -hatched kingsnakes often cycle with just a short period of cooling rather than hibernation. When California kingsnakes are well fed, maintain a good body weight, and are properly cycled, they will breed annually. Captives may have up to three clutches of four to twelve eggs. If a third clutch is produced, it is usually the smallest and is apt to contain one or more infertile eggs. Female kingsnakes differ from males in having a more slender and shorter tail. The tail of the male is heavy near the cloaca and quite long. Sexes are easily determined by probing (see page 55 for additional details). Hatchlings look very much like the adults.

Other Snakes with Similar Needs

Other subspecies of the eastern kingsnake will thrive when kept as outlined for the California kingsnake. However, some subspecies are larger than the California kingsnake and will require larger cages when adult. Prairie and mole kingsnakes (*Lampropeltis calligaster* ssp.) will also do well when kept in a similar manner.

Variable Kingsnake
Lampropeltis mexicana

Description

This beautiful and variable-colored and -patterned snake occurs in central Mexico. Within the last decade it has become a very popular pet trade snake. Although no longer differentiated by subspecies by taxonomists, hobbyists continue to divide this snake into several phases.

• The "mexicana phase" is also referred to by hobbyists as the San Luis Potosi kingsnake. This is often a gray snake with black-edged carmine saddles.

• The "greeri phase" is known by herpetoculturists as the Durango Mountain kingsnake. It has a light gray ground color and the dark saddles may be black or mostly black with red centers.

• The term "leonis or Nuevo Leon phase" is used by hobbyists to describe the snakes with a peach, tan, or buckskin ground color and orange-red saddles that are narrowly edged with black.

• The "thayeri phase" known by hobbyists is the most variable, varying from a black, red, and white (sometimes yellowish)-ringed milksnake pattern on one end of the

Variable kingsnakes occur in many colors and patterns. This is a milksnake phase.

spectrum to snakes having very reduced patterns on the other.

• Albinism and melanism have been documented.

Size and Lifespan

A smaller species, the variable kingsnake is adult at lengths between 26 and 36 inches (66–91 cm). Individuals have lived for more than 15 years in captivity.

Range

This is a snake of semiarid elevations in the Mexican states of Coahuila, Durango, Guanajuato, Nuevo Leon, San Luis Potosi, Tamaulipas, and Zacatecas. Variable kingsnakes are often associated with rocky outcroppings, escarpments, and other regions of fissured rocks.

Captive Care

Until a few years ago, when herpetoculturists began seriously working with this little snake, it was seldom available and when it was, it was very costly. It is not that it is a rare snake, but because Mexico now protects all of its wildlife, it was difficult for snake breeders to acquire enough stock to produce sufficient babies for the American pet trade.

This phase is referred to as the "Mex–Mex" phase by hobbyists.

However, over time, the numbers of variable kingsnakes have increased, and prices have dropped.

In the wild, the diet of this small, supple kingsnake contains a high percentage of lizards. However, captives usually eat small prekilled rodents readily.

The cage must be clean, dry, and provide a thermal gradient. A temperature of from 87°F (30.5°C) on the warm end to 70 to 80°F (21–26°C) on the cool end of the terrarium should be provided. A single adult variable kingsnake can be maintained in a 15-gallon (56.7-L) terrarium (12 × 12 × 24 inches [30 × 30 × 61 cm]), and a pair in a 20-gallon (75.7-L) long terrarium (12 × 12 × 30 inches [30 × 30 × 76 cm]).

Babies, which should be maintained separately, can be kept in much smaller terraria.

This is a secretive snake that seems to feel most secure if provided with a substrate into which it can burrow, as well as one or two hideboxes. They seldom voluntarily climb. A dish of clean drinking water is mandatory, but if your snake routinely uses it to soak in for long periods of time, reduce the size of the dish until it can no longer do so. When startled, these snakes may strike. Handle them carefully.

Breeding

Variable kingsnakes require a 10- to 12-week period of hibernation to cycle reproductively. These snakes

A "leonis" phase variable kingsnake.

will breed annually. A clutch normally contains between four and twelve eggs. Female variable kingsnakes have more slender and shorter tails than the males. Sexes are easily determined by probing (see page 55 for additional details). Hatchlings look very much like the adults.

Other Snakes with Similar Needs

Related kingsnakes, such as the gray-banded kingsnake, *L. alterna*, of western Texas and the Queretaro kingsnake, *L. ruthveni*, of northcentral Mexico are also hardy, pretty species. Both are about the same size as the variable kingsnake and may be maintained in a similar manner. Hatchling gray-banded kingsnakes may not readily accept pinky mice for

their first few meals. Before purchase, be certain that any gray-banded kingsnakes you are hoping to acquire are feeding voluntarily on readily available prey.

The "greeri" phase of the variable kingsnake is gray with narrow red bands.

Honduran Milksnake
Lampropeltis triangulum hondurensis

Description

There are at least 35 forms (species and subspecies) of tricolored king- and milksnakes available to hobbyists today. Of all, the Honduran milksnake has emerged as the clear favorite and is now produced by the hundreds each year in a number of color and pattern variations. Known for its color diversity in the wild, close to a dozen designer colors have been established by breeders.

Wild Morphs

• Tricolored. This, the typical milk-snake phase, is ringed with red, black, and white (or yellow). Babies are very brilliantly colored, but with growth and age, black tipping occurs on both the white and the red scales, dulling the snake's initial brilliance considerably. Albinos of this pattern morph are now readily available, but are still much more expensive than the normally colored examples.
• Tangerine. This is a red, orange, and black on orange color phase. All colors (except the black) vary in intensity. Black scale tipping may be present, but is largely lacking on the brightest-colored specimens. Albino tangerines are available, but are expensive.

An albino Honduran milksnake.

• Bicolored. This broad-banded black and red color phase is the least colorful of the morphs. Although the red may be quite bright when the snake is young, all red scales are usually tipped extensively with black pigment. Typically, the amount of black increases as the snake ages.

Designer Morphs

• Albino tricolor. This is a typically colored albino, banded in creamy white and orange against a hazy strawberry red. It was once formidably expensive but is now dropping rapidly in price.
• Albino tangerine. This beautiful snake is banded in wide and narrow bands of orange separated by narrow bands of white
• Hybino. This is a combination of the hypomelanistic and the albino morphs. It is rosy orange in color and the black bands have imprecise edges.
• Peach. The orange coloration has peach overtones.
• Snow. This very pale Honduran combines the genetics of the albino and the anerythristic morphs.
• Ghost. Even paler than the snow morph, the ghost is produced by crossing a hypomelanistic Honduran with an anerythristic.

A brilliantly colored normal phase Honduran milksnake.

• Disappearing pattern. This hazy orange-red milksnake has thin black markings when hatched but these fade (almost to oblivion) as the creature grows.
• Hypomelanistic. This Honduran morph has reduced black pigment.
• Anerythristic. This is a dark morph that lacks red pigment.

Other terms such as striped, pin-striped, and chain refer to the width or appearance of the dark banding. The terms heterozygous, double heterozygous, or triple heterozygous indicate that although the snake is of one color combination, it is carrying masked genes for an alternate expression of color. When a pair of triple heterozygous Honduran milksnakes is bred together, any or all colors and patterns may be produced in a single clutch of eggs.

This snake has a narrow head, is slender when young, but is quite heavy bodied when adult. The tangerine morph and its designer derivatives retain much of their brightness throughout their lives. However, the normally pigmented tricolored and bicolored morphs darken, often very noticeably, as they age.

Size and Lifespan

A length of 4 to 5.5 feet (122–165 cm) is normally attained by captive adults. A lifespan of between 12 and 18 years can be expected.

Range

The Honduran milksnake occurs at low elevations in a variety of habitats in Nicaragua, Honduras, and possibly in extreme northeastern Costa Rica. Like all milksnakes, this is a secretive snake that despite its size, is easily overlooked.

Captive Care

The Honduran milksnake is one of the larger of the 25 races. It usually feeds readily on lab mice, and hatchlings are large enough to eat pinky mice.

The caging for Honduran milksnakes must be clean and dry. If their cage is allowed to become damp and unclean, these milksnakes will develop blister disease syndrome (see page 30). A thermal gradient providing a temperature of about 87°F (30.5°C) on the warm end to 70 to 80°F (21–26.6°C) on the cool end is ideal. Cage humidity should be moderate. A single large adult Honduran milksnake can be maintained in a 20-gallon (75.7-L) long terrarium (12 × 12 × 30 inches [30 × 30 × 78 cm]). A pair should have a 40-gallon (151-L) "breeder" tank (these vary in size by manufacturer, but are usually in the 18 × 16 × 36-inch [46 × 41 × 91-cm] range). Babies can be maintained in much smaller terraria, but because they can be cannibalistic, it is better to keep the babies separately.

Like all milksnakes, Hondurans are very secretive. They should be provided with a substrate into which they can burrow (aspen shavings or Carefresh bedding are excellent choices) as well as one or two hide-boxes. Visual barriers such as limbs or rocks on the floor of the cage will also help provide a feeling of security. A dish of clean drinking water is mandatory and will help provide a higher cage humidity. If your snake routinely uses this for long soaks, reduce the size of the dish. Honduran milksnakes will bite if startled and are often very "wiggly" when handled. Some may press their nose against the side of your hand or a finger and then quickly bite and chew. Handle them carefully and remain alert.

Breeding

The vast majority of the Honduran milksnakes now available to hobbyists are captive bred and captive hatched. They cycle best for breeding if hibernated (brumated) for an eight- to twelve-week period during our winter months. A healthy Honduran milksnake with adequate body

This is an anerythristic Honduran milksnake.

weight will have either one or two clutches of eggs annually. A clutch typically contains between three and twelve eggs; the second clutch is often the smaller of the two. Female milksnakes differ from males in having a more slender and shorter tail. Sexes are easily determined by probing (see page 55 for additional details). Hatchlings look very much like the adults in pattern, but usually lack black scale tipping.

Other Snakes with Similar Needs

The husbandry regimen suggested for the Honduran milksnake is equally suitable for the other races of the milksnake, as well as for the various mountain kingsnakes. Many of the milksnakes and mountain kingsnakes from the United States are considerably smaller when adult than the Honduran milksnake. These small forms may be kept in smaller cages.

Rosy Boa
Charina trivirgata

Description

Four subspecies of this little constrictor are currently recognized. The Mexican and the Mid-Baja rosy boas are usually easily different from the coastal and the desert rosy boas, but characteristics of the latter two may overlap considerably. Where subspecies abut, intergradation can occur.

• The coastal rosy boa, *C. t. roseofusca*, is found from southeastern California to northwestern Baja California. This subspecies tends to have striping with uneven (almost ragged) edges. The stripes may be pale rose, deep tan, or orange against a ground color of gray. The lateral stripes may be darker than the vertebral stripe. Some degree of speckling (often profuse) of the same color as the stripes is present between the stripes. The ground color is gray. In some areas these boas may lack even vestiges of definite striping. Despite the fact that there is usually a small but varying amount of orangish pigment on the back and sides, because of the lack of precise markings these boas are referred to by hobbyists as "unicolored." Albinos and hypomelanistic

An example of the desert phase of rosy boa from near Wickenburg, Arizona.

examples of the coastal rosy boa are now well known. These are variably patterned, having from sparse to moderate orange striping and speckling on an off-white ground color.

• The desert rosy boa, *C. t. gracia*, can be confusingly similar to the coastal rosy boa in appearance. The desert rosy boa occurs eastward from southcentral California to central western Arizona. Although it has an extensive overall range, the actual populations, associated with aridland canyons, are widely scattered and many have developed characteristic colors. This beautiful snake has rather even-edged brown to russet stripes on a gray ground color. Arizona examples tend to be very richly colored.

• The Central Baja rosy boa, *C. t. saslowi*, of southern and central Baja California Norte has well-defined, straight-edged orange to russet stripes against a steel gray ground color. This is the form often referred to as "myriolepis" (an invalid subspecies name) by dealers and hobbyists. It is considered one of the most beautiful of the rosy boas and is in great demand by hobbyists.

• The Mexican rosy boa, *C. t. trivirgata*, occurs in northwestern Sonora,

This is a pretty coastal-phase rosy boa from the vicinity of Borrego Springs, California.

Mexico, on the southern Baja Peninsula, on Isla Cedros, and in south-central Arizona. Although it is the darkest of the four races, it is pleasantly colored and is very popular with hobbyists. The chocolate to nearly black stripes have even edges and contrast strongly with the cream to pale tan ground color.

Size and Lifespan

The four subspecies of rosy boa vary in adult size from 20 to 42 inches (51–107 cm) in length. All subspecies are moderately stocky. Adult males are noticeably smaller than adult females. The Mexican and the Mid-Baja rosy boas are the smallest subspecies. Longevity of more than 15 years is not uncommon for this snake.

Range

In one or another of its subspecies, the rosy boa is found from southern California to central Arizona, then southward to central Sonora and throughout the Baja Peninsula. In some areas the boas may be widespread and easily found; in others they are very locally distributed. Rosy boas are associated with rocky terrain and although they may occur well away from water sources, they seem most common where at least a little surface water is available.

Captive Care

Because they are small, easily handled, affordable, hardy, and colorful, rosy boas are fast becoming one of America's favorite snake

This coastal phase rosy boa is of typical pattern and color.

species. Although all of the races will interbreed readily, advanced herpetoculturists are almost fanatical about maintaining locale-specific (to a specific canyon, in some cases) breeding programs.

In all but perpetually humid areas, rosy boas are wonderfully hardy little boas. However, in areas where there is perpetually high humidity, unless their cage humidity is kept low, rosy boas may occasionally develop a difficult-to-correct regurgitation syndrome. Although proper husbandry—suitably warm temperature, low cage humidity, and prey of proper size—may correct this in its early stages, if left untreated, the snakes can weaken and die.

Because rosy boas are small and relatively inactive, they do not require particularly large cages. A single snake, or a pair, of average adult size may be kept in a 15- to 20-gallon (57–76-L) terrarium (12 × 12 × 24 or 12 × 12 × 30 inches [30 × 30 × 61 cm or 30 × 30 × 76 cm], respectively). Since rosy boas are adept at pushing terrarium tops off, the terrarium top must be of a clip-on or lock-on style. Despite the fact that rosy boas inhabit aridland habitats, they are not truly snakes of sandy areas. Rather, they are more closely associated with areas of rocky desert scrub and canyonlands. They will avidly burrow in loose sand, but utilize rodent burrows extensively. Because sand is apt to get in the mouth of captive rosy boas while they are burrowing or eating, newspaper, paper towels,

This is a Mexican rosy boa from the southern Baja Peninsula.

or aspen shavings are a more appropriate cage substrate.

Rosy boas are usually very easy to handle but they do develop an avid feeding response. If you have the smell of mice on your fingers when you approach them they may attempt to bite. The answer to this potential problem is simple: Wash your hands before handling your boa.

Breeding

Because of their stubby tails, it can be difficult to sex rosy boas at a glance. Males do have a slightly longer tail, are smaller than adult females when adult, and usually have cloacal spurs that are noticeably larger than those of the females; however, probing is the most conclusive method of sexing these snakes. Once it is ascertained that you actually have a pair, with just a little attention to winter

cycling, acclimated rosy boas are very easily bred in captivity. Males may become sexually mature a year (or even more) earlier than the females. Healthy female rosy boas can produce their litter of large, live babies annually.

Rosy boas normally hibernate during the winter months, so this is the most successful way of cycling the snakes for breeding. A drop from their normally warm summer temperature to 48–54°F (8.9–12°C) for a period of eight to ten weeks usually suffices to condition the snakes for breeding. During the period of reduced temperature most hobbyists also darken the cage around the clock. Before being hibernated (the new word for this is "brumated"), your snake must be allowed to empty its gut. Do not feed it for at least two weeks before placing it in the hibernaculum; however, the snake should be allowed to drink whenever it chooses. It is probably prudent to rouse your snake about halfway through its hibernation cycle and provide it an opportunity to drink.

After the passing of the eight to ten weeks of hibernation, increase the photoperiod, temperature, and relative humidity in the cage. This can be done gradually or at one time, as you prefer. After the boas are active again, feed them, place them together (if you keep them separately), and hope for the best.

It is very important to have the snakes in excellent condition before lowering temperatures, for the snakes eat only reluctantly throughout the actual breeding season. In our experience, it has not mattered whether the boas are kept together throughout the year or introduced only at breeding time.

Provide gravid female rosy boas with a temperature gradient. Although room temperature should be adequate for the cool end of the terrarium, a basking hot spot on the substrate surface of from 85–95°F (29–35°C) is ideal. This will allow the gravid female to choose the temperature most suitable for the developing young. Improper cage temperatures can result in aborted, undeveloped egg masses or partially developed or deformed young. Even a short period of improper temperature can result in aberrant patterns or other (usually unwanted) abnormalities.

If born late in the year, some neonate rosy boas may refuse to eat. Hobbyists have learned that if these holdouts are put into hibernation for several weeks, when they are warmed, the babies often feed readily and grow rapidly.

Other Snakes with Similar Needs

There are no other closely related snakes that have the same regimen of care as the rosy boas.

East African Sand Boa

Eryx colubrinus

Description

Although hobbyists continue to differentiate the Kenyan examples of this boa as *E. c. loveridgei*, systematists are no longer recognizing subspecies of this pretty East African snake. Typically, the ground color varies from pale tan through buff to bright orange. Against this are large, dark, dorsal blotches. The belly is off-white to immaculate white. The more southerly examples tend to be brighter. The morph referred to as the Dodona phase has enhanced areas of orange and reduced dark markings. Some examples are overall reddish brown to chocolate and lack most, if not all, contrasting markings. This variant is referred to as the **rufescens morph** and is occasionally advertised as *Eryx colubrinus rufescens*. The snout is shovel-shaped, perfect for digging in loose soil or forcing their way along rodent tunnels. Posteriorly, the scales of the East African sand boa are very heavily keeled. The tail is conical.

Amelanistic (lacking black pigment), anerythristic (lacking red color), and snow phases are now being bred in ever-increasing num-

A normally colored and patterned East African sand boa.

bers. The paradox sand boa is a snow phase with variable black markings.

Size and Lifespan

Adult females of this secretive aridland and savannah snake may be slightly in excess of 30 inches (76 cm) in length. Males are usually substantially smaller. These boas have lived for more than 15 years in captivity.

Range

Although the East African sand boa occurs over a vast area of East Africa, most imported into the United States originate in Tanzania or Kenya. Those from Tanzania tend to have more subtle, lighter colors than the bright orange and brown examples from Kenya.

Captive Care

Because of their small size, sand boas, in general, do well in rather small terraria. A 20-gallon (75.7-L) long terrarium is sufficiently large to house a pair, a trio, or even two pairs (male sand boas are not seriously territorial) of adults of almost any species. A fairly deep substrate of fine sand or dry mulch will provide a suitable habitat. A heating pad or a heat tape should be placed beneath

The orange on the naturally occurring "flame" East African sand boa is brighter and more extensive than that of the normal.

one end of the terrarium. This will provide a thermal gradient from which the snakes can choose the most suitable substrate temperatures. A daytime temperature of 92–100°F (33–37.7°C) on the hot end is desirable. The cool end can be "room temperature." Temperatures can be allowed to drop several degrees at night. Gravid female erycines should have the option of remaining warm around the clock.

Because East African sand boas metabolize much of their moisture requirements from their food animals, it is not necessary (or even desirable) for a water bowl to be continually present. However, they should be offered water for a few hours every two days. Daytime temperatures ranging from mid-80–mid

90°F (27–37°C) are ideal. A nighttime drop into low 70°F or high 60°F (21 or 20.5°C) is entirely acceptable.

Captive sand boas don't need either a sand substrate or a naturalistic terrarium to thrive. In fact, many very successful breeders suggest that sand or soil substrates may eventually lead to intestinal impactions and advocate a substrate of newspaper, paper towels, or aspen shavings, used in conjunction with one or more hideboxes. Certainly all of these artificial substrates will suffice and are very easily changed or spot-cleaned when necessary. Many breeders also use plastic shoe, sweater, or blanket boxes with snap-on lids or racks designed specifically to hold them rather than glass terraria or cages. The choice is yours, and the variations

This all-brown morph of the East African sand boa is often referred to as the "rufescens" morph.

are many. Because tightly closed caging receptacles build up far too much internal humidity for sand boas, if you use covered plastic boxes it will usually be necessary to drill or melt (with a soldering iron) ventilation holes into several of the sides. Be certain that the holes are not large enough to allow the boas to escape.

However, with that now said, we must mention that we advocate naturalistic terraria and have maintained and bred sand boas of several species for years on sand-soil substrates. We have never once had problems with gut impactions of any sort. It just may be that not all sand is created equal. For example, the sharp silica play sand available in garden stores may not pass through a boa's intestinal tract as readily as

smooth desert sand does. But again, we have used both without ill effects.

Sand boas having 2 to 3 inches (5–7.6 cm) of a sand-soil mixture, plus cage furniture such as rocks and limbs, may be so much at home that they seldom surface. If heavy cage furniture (rocks, limbs, etc.) is used, it must be placed directly on the bottom of the tank and affixed in place. This is a particularly important step, for if these items are not secured, your boas are apt to burrow beneath them and be injured. Once the heavy furniture is in place, add the several inches of smooth-grained sand. If you choose to add drought-tolerant plants (spineless or nearly spineless cacti, *Astrophytum*, among them, and succulents such as those of the genus *Haworthia*),

Designer morphs (such as this albino) of the East African sand boa are now readily available.

the plants that you have chosen can be left right in their pots and sunk, pot and all, into the sand. The periodic watering of these plants will provide a bit of humidity and temporary moistening of the sand but, if in moderation, this should do no harm. Manzanita branches or cholla (cactus) skeletons can also be added.

Heat can be provided on one end of the terrarium by either an under-tank heater or an overhead light. Added heat may be especially important for a gravid female. The top should clip or lock tightly in place. An incandescent (full-spectrum is not necessary but will do no harm) light fixture and directed-beam bulb will be needed for the plants if not for the boas.

A bit of periodic subsurface moisture may be beneficial. If you have several inches of sand, accomplishing this is a simple feat. Merely push a hollow length of PVC through the sand to the bottom of the tank. Once it is in position, slowly—the keyword here is slowly—*trickle* the desired amount of water into the standpipe. The water will percolate along the bottom of the tank, dampening the bottommost layers of sand while leaving the upper layers perfectly dry. Your erycines can then choose the substrate moisture level best suited to them.

Breeding

East African sand boas breed in spring and early summer. Provide gravid female sand boas with a tem-

New color variations of the East African sand boa are being continually developed. This very orange example was bred by Brian Emanuel.

perature gradient. Although room temperature should be adequate for the cool end of the terrarium, a basking hot spot on the substrate surface of from 85–95°F (29–35°C) should be provided. This will allow the gravid female to choose the temperature most suitable for the developing babies.

A litter may contain from three to twenty-two rather large, live babies. These are born in the fall. If kept sufficiently warm, the neonates usually accept newborn mice readily. A very occasional neonate may prefer lizards rather than mice for its first meal(s). These holdouts will soon switch to pinkies if the mice are scented with lizard odor.

The East African sand boa is a very robust and hardy species. They breed most reliably if gently cooled during the winter months but do not need a period of complete hibernation.

Other Snakes with Similar Needs

A sand boa of almost any other species would also be an excellent choice. Most are about the same size when adults as the East African sand boa. Among those most commonly seen are the rough-scaled sand boa, *Eryx conicus*, the West African sand boa, *Eryx muelleri*, and the smooth-scaled sand boa, *Eryx johnii.* Russian sand boas, *Eryx miliaris*, are often available and are of interest to hobbyists because of their varied colors. Cinnamons, variable tans, and black are common colors of the Russian sand boa. Of the species mentioned, the smooth-scaled sand boa is the largest and would require a larger terrarium than we discussed in the captive care section above. A minimum terrarium size of 50 gallons (189 L) would be suggested for this sand boa species.

Ball Python

Python regius

Description

This is another of the snakes that are now available not only in an inexpensive normal coloration, but in 15 to 20 designer colors (some very costly) as well. Normal-colored ball pythons are now farmed in large numbers in various West African countries. Eggs from captive females are collected and hatched, and the hatchlings are then exported.

Perhaps, as much because they are inexpensive as for the mystique that continues to be associated with owning a python, ball pythons have become immensely popular in the pet trade. The normal-colored ball python (the wild morph) has an intricate, but usually regular, pattern of brown lateral blotches that contrast prettily against a ground color of tan or buff. Pastels, albinos, caramels, and several other colors have now been developed through selective breeding. Here are a few examples of these designer colors:

• Piebald: Otherwise normal and colors and patterns are interrupted by random spots or rings of pure white.
• Albino: Golden-ocher spots contrast sharply with a white ground color.

A ball python in a characteristic pose.

• Lavender albino: The colors on this almost pastel morph are far less contrasting. The dark spots are creamy yellow against a ground color of pale lavender.
• Pinstriped: The dark markings have been reduced to a tracery of lines against a gold-brown ground color.
• Clown: The dark markings are reduced, fragmented, and irregular.
• Lemon pastel: Rather than tan or buff, the light areas are lemony yellow.
• Genetic striped: Rather than having been caused by irregular incubation temperatures, this morph has a genetically replicable yellow vertebral stripe and very reduced dark markings.
• Leucistic: Pure white, black eyes, no markings.
• Super cinnamon: Nearly black with obscure markings.
• Ghost, ivory, spider, and caramel are just a few more designer designations.

Ball pythons are usually quiet snakes that, when startled, will coil into a tight ball, the head in a protected position in the center. In Europe the same snake is known as the **royal python**, the name being derived from the specific name of *regius*.

There are now so many designer morphs of the ball python available that it is difficult to name some. This is a pastel.

Size and Lifespan

3.5 to 6 feet (1.1–1.8 m) is the normal size range for adult ball pythons. A very occasional example may near 7 feet (2.1 m) in length. The very heavy girth of this snake makes it look considerably larger than it actually is. Although a longevity of more than 50 years has been reported for this snake, between 15 and 25 years is the more common.

Natural Range

This small python inhabits tropical dry forests and savannas throughout much of tropical West and tropical Central Africa.

Captive Care

Because they may be reluctant to eat, wild-collected ball pythons can be very problematic snakes. However, captive-bred babies that are feeding well are very easily maintained and may even be con-

sidered an excellent beginners' choice.

Ball pythons are shy snakes and are usually quite inactive; they do not require a particularly large cage. A baby or two can be started and partially grown in a terrarium of only 10-gallon (38-L) capacity. One or two average-sized adults will require a terrarium of 40- to 50-gallon (151–189-L) capacity, or a cage of similar size. Although ball pythons can climb, and occasionally will do so, providing climbing limbs is optional. An elevated shelf is actually more functional. A substrate of cypress bark mulch, aspen shavings, or newspaper should be provided. Fresh water should be available at all times. One hidebox or more should be included in any caging setup. Cages that provide a thermal gradient and a cage temperature ranging between 80°F (26.6°C) (cool end) and 90°F (32°C) (hot end) seems ideal. Cage humidity should be high, in case the snakes have difficulty shedding their skin.

Breeding

Because male ball pythons are quite apt to fast during the breeding season, it is imperative that their weight be optimal at the onset. Females may fast, but seem less apt to do so. If pythons will eat, even occasionally, during the breeding season, it will be to their benefit. A period of cooling—just cooling, not hibernation!—to a low nighttime temperature of about 70°F (21°C) (daytime highs should still be 80–89°F [27–31.6°C]) during the winter (short photoperiod days) will help cycle ball pythons for breeding.

Because they are a short-tailed species, ball pythons may be difficult to sex by using external characters. However, sexes are easily determined by probing (see page 55 for additional details).

Ball pythons breed from late October to late in the winter during the period of winter cooling. Most breeders introduce the males to the female's cage. Female ball pythons oviposit in early spring. These snakes have small clutches (usually three to eight eggs) of large eggs. Incubation takes about two months. Hatchling ball pythons are much like the adults in appearance. Color and pattern intensity of both juveniles and adults is almost identical. However, for their 10-inch (25-cm) length the hatchlings are a little more slender and they have a proportionately larger head.

Albino ball pythons were among the first of the genetic "sports."

Other Snakes with Similar Needs

Both smaller and larger species of pythons and some boas will thrive when provided a husbandry regimen such as previously described. Research the species in question carefully. Cage size may need to be either larger or smaller and temperature may need to be a bit warmer overall.

This is a clown morph ball python.

Common Garter Snake

Thamnophis sirtalis ssp.

Description

There are 12 subspecies of the common garter snake. They are of both Eastern and Western distribution. One, the San Francisco garter snake, *T. s. tetrataenia*, a beautiful snake with vivid yellow, orange, and black stripes, is a federally endangered species and must not be collected or otherwise molested.

Many of the more brightly colored subspecies and morphs of the common garter snake are now being bred in captivity. These include the red-spotted, the California red-sided, albino eastern, and black eastern garter snakes.

The two races of common garter snake with the largest ranges are the eastern, *T. s. sirtalis*, and the Plains red-sided, *T. s. parietalis*. The former varies immensely in coloration and pattern. They are usually prominently patterned in three stripes of bright yellow. However, the stripes may be tan, buff, orange, or lacking. If lacking, the pattern is usually of prominent checks instead.

• From the proximity of Lake Erie comes a morph of the eastern garter snake that is almost solid

A flame morph of the eastern garter snake has now been developed and stabilized.

black and patternless. Albinism is well documented.

• The Maritime garter snake, *T. s. pallidula*, is very much like the eastern, but is usually darker. Island populations may be brightly colored and checkered rather than spotted.

• The Chicago garter snake, *T. s. semifasciata*, is striped, but has a checkered neck pattern.

• The Plains red-sided garter snake, *T. s. parietalis*, is also variable. The vertebral stripe is usually very prominent but the lateral stripes are less so. Between these, along the upper sides, are alternating black and red spots.

• The New Mexico garter snake, *T. s. dorsalis*, is similar to the Plains red-sided but is of overall duller coloration.

• The blue-striped garter snake, *T. s. similis*, is aptly named. Against the black ground color are three stripes that vary from bluish white to vivid blue. It is a pretty snake that is becoming more popular with hobbyists.

• The California red-sided garter snake, *T. s. infernalis*, and the red-spotted garter snake, *T. s. concinnus*, are both Pacific Coast races. The top of the head of both is red. The former is the brighter of the two,

The Oregon red-spotted garter snake, T. s. concinna, *is among the most beautiful of the taxa.*

having a bluish white to yellow vertebral stripe, light lateral stripes, and bright red spots alternating with black on the upper sides.

• The red-spotted garter snake is mostly black on the sides with discrete red (sometimes yellow) spots.
• The Puget Sound garter snake, *T. s. pickeringii* is black with three yellow stripes.
• The Valley garter snake is very variable in color, but is usually prominently striped, has some red on the sides, and the top of the head is dark.

Size and Lifespan

Some subspecies of the common garter snake have measured more than 4 feet (1.2 m) in length. However, a length of between 18 and 36 inches (46–91 cm) is more common. A longevity of 10 years is not uncommon, and some captives have lived for more than 15 years.

Natural Range

The common garter snake is represented in the United States by a number of subspecies. These range southward from the Canadian Provinces to Florida and Texas in the East and Southwest (there is also a subspecies that is found in New Mexico) and from southern Alaska to southern California in the West. They are absent from most of the western plains and desert states.

Captive Care

The various races of the common garter snake are easily kept and are very hardy. However, like most snakes that eat ectothermic prey, garter snakes metabolize their food quickly and stool frequently; their cage, therefore, requires frequent cleaning. Garter snakes are members of the water snake group. They must always have fresh water avail-

A normal eastern garter snake.

able, but their substrate must be dry. Cage humidity should be moderately high or garter snakes may have difficulty shedding their skin. These snakes may soak often and sometimes for rather long periods in their water bowl, and may stool in the water as well. Be certain that their water remains fresh and clean.

A thermal gradient should be provided. Room temperature (68–80°F [20–27°C]) is suitable for the cool end of the cage, but an illuminated basking area of 85 to 90°F (29–32°C) is suggested.

Until they are fully acclimated, common garter snakes may be nervous and they will always be secretive. From one to several baby garter snakes, which are 6 to 9 inches (15–23 cm) long at birth, can be maintained in a 10-gallon (38-L) terrarium. However, an adult should have a terrarium of no less than 15-

gallon (56.7-L) capacity, and a pair or trio should have a terrarium of from 20 gallons (75.7 L) (12 × 12 × 30 inches [20 × 20 × 76 cm]) to 50 gallons (189 L) in size.

Since garter snakes seldom climb, the height of the terrarium need be no greater than 12 or 14 inches (30–36 cm). Visual barriers such as plants, rocks, limbs, and hiding spots should be incorporated into the terrarium design. Keep in mind that garter snakes will burrow, and any cage furniture provided should be secured to prevent it from settling on top of, and injuring or killing, the snake. This caution is especially important in the case of heavy rocks or limbs.

Until they become used to gentle handling, garter snakes may not only bite in defense—this may make one or several pinpoint breaks of the skin—when restrained but *will* smear

An albino eastern garter snake.

musk and feces on their handlers. Both of these defensive ploys are discomfiting. Wash your hands carefully. With frequent gentle handling your garter snake will soon desist employing these defensive tactics.

The dietary preferences of these snakes vary geographically. Those from the plains and the west will readily eat pinky mice as well as worms, slugs, minnows, tadpoles, frogs, and toads. However, the eastern races may refuse nestling rodents but will readily eat the same invertebrate and amphibian fare.

Breeding

Garter snakes are live-bearing, and large females may have astonishingly large clutches—more than 75 babies have been recorded in a given clutch. The neonates are similar in pattern to the adults, but are usually paler in color and appear to have proportionately large heads. Babies vary from 5 to 9 inches (12.7–23 cm) in length at birth.

Since common garter snakes normally hibernate during the winter months, simulating hibernation is the most successful way of cycling the snakes for breeding. A drop from their normally warm summer temperature to 48–54°F (8.9–12°C) for a period of eight to ten weeks usually suffices to condition the snakes for breeding. During the period of reduced temperature it also seems best to darken the cage around the clock. Before being hibernated ("brumated") your snake must be allowed to empty its gut. Do not feed it for about a week and a half before placing it in the hibernaculum; however, the snake should be allowed to drink whenever it

The red-sided garter snake is a beautifully colored plains form of the common garter snake.

chooses. It is probably prudent to rouse your snake about halfway through its hibernation cycle and provide it an opportunity to drink.

After the passing of the eight to ten weeks of hibernation, increase the photoperiod, temperature, and relative humidity in the cage. This can be done gradually or all at once, as you prefer. After the garter snakes are active again, feed them, place them together (if you keep them separately) and hope for the best.

Hibernation is stressful for reptiles. It is, therefore, very important to have the snakes in excellent condition before lowering temperatures. Hobbyists seem to have equal luck whether the snakes are kept together throughout the year or are brought together only at breeding time.

It is very important that you provide gravid female garter snakes with a temperature gradient. Doing so will allow the gravid female to choose the temperature most suitable for her developing young. Improper cage temperatures can result in aborted undeveloped egg masses or partially developed or deformed young. Even a short period of improper temperature may result in aberrant patterns or other (usually unwanted) abnormalities.

Other Snakes with Similar Needs

Ribbon snakes, ground snakes, lined snakes, brown snakes, red-bellied snakes, and ring-necked snakes will all do well when provided with the above caging conditions. However, some do have different feeding preferences so be sure to thoroughly research the species you intend to keep.

Brown House Snake

Lamprophis fuliginosus

Description

Although there are about a dozen species in this genus, only the brown house snake has gained popularity with hobbyists. Usually a rich brown in color, this snake may also be tan to terra-cotta above. No matter what the dorsal coloration is, it is opalescent white below. The terra-cotta morph is eagerly sought by hobbyists. A pair of light (white to pinkish) facial stripes are often the only contrasting marks. Albinos are now established. The pupils are vertically elliptical, attesting to a nocturnal activity pattern. Despite its small size, this is a supple and strong constrictor.

Size and Lifespan

16 to 40 inches (41–102 cm). Adult females are conspicuously larger than adult males. A lifespan of between 12 and 15 years is commonly attained.

Natural Range

This snake is of wide distribution in sub-Saharan Africa. Most of the examples now in the pet trade are coming from southern Africa and East Africa.

Cheryl Bott breeds many albino brown house snakes.

Captive Care

The brown house snake is a very easily maintained species. Because they are small and not overly active, a pair of brown house snakes can be maintained in a 10- to 15-gallon (38- to 57-L) capacity terrarium. House snakes inhabit sparsely vegetated, rock-strewn, semi-arid, and aridland habitats. Their terrarium should be based on this concept, being of comparatively low humidity, and containing visual barriers, a dry substrate, and a dish of fresh water. House snakes are secretive, and will often burrow into or beneath the cage substrate. To prevent the injury or death of the snake, make certain that no heavy cage furniture can move and accidentally settle on top of a burrowing snake. A corkbark hide or a plastic hidebox will be readily used by your house snakes. The substrate may be aspen or pine shavings, newspaper, or other such easily cleaned medium.

In the wild these snakes accept lizards, frogs, and small rodents. They can usually be acclimated to, and will thrive on, a diet of lab mice.

House snakes vary in disposition, but most do not bite if they are handled carefully. Until tame, however, they will often void the contents of

Hobbyists eagerly seek the reddest morphs of the brown house snake.

their cloaca, smearing musk and feces on their handler. This disconcerting defensive ploy is typical of a great many snake species.

Breeding

The brown house snake is an amazingly fecund species and will often breed in captivity with very little preparation. Although a short period of cooling may help to cycle these snakes reproductively, the cooling does not seem mandatory. A female may produce four or more clutches containing from three to eighteen (usually between six and ten) eggs annually at intervals of about two months. Since gravid

females may refuse food for the second half of each gestation period, it is easier to maintain your female in good condition if she is limited to two clutches of eggs and then is rested. Females differ from males in being considerably larger and in having a more slender and shorter tail. Sexes are easily determined by probing (see page 55 for additional details).

The eggs should be incubated at a temperature of about 80°F (27°C). The incubation duration is usually nine to ten weeks.

Hatchling house snakes are quite small (6 to 8 inches [15–20 cm] in total length) and look very much like the adults. Following their first shed, they will usually eat newly born lab mice readily.

Other Snakes with Similar Needs

Occasionally a few other species of house snakes are available. Among those more easily kept are the spotted (*L. guttatus*), "Kilamanjaro" (*L. fuliginosus* ssp.), and olive (*L. inornatus*) house snakes. The very pretty and coveted aurora house (*L. aurora*) snake can be difficult to acclimate; it is not a good choice for most hobbyists.

A profile of a brown house snake. Note the elliptical pupils.

This dark house snake from Mt. Kilimanjaro has extensive white lines.

Leopard Gecko
Eublepharis macularius

Description

Leopard geckos are pretty, adapt well to terraria as small as 10 or 15 gallons (37.8–57 L) in size, are very hardy, and require little specialized support equipment. In short, there could hardly be a better lizard species for beginning hobbyists, and, today, leopard geckos come in enough "designer colors" to hold the interest of their keepers through intermediate and extended interest stages as well.

The leopard gecko is in the lizard family Eublepharidae. This is a primitive family containing primarily terrestrial members that share such characteristics as having well-developed and fully functional eyelids (geckos in other families lack eyelids), and that lack the toepads so typical of many of the geckos in the family Gekkonidae. The eublepharine geckos have vertically elliptical pupils, which expand greatly in the darkness.

All eublepharines have the caudal (tail) scales arranged in prominent whorls. There is often a basal constriction, at which point their tail breaks rather easily. The tail regrows (regenerates) quickly but the regen-

The precise banding of young leopard geckos diffuses with growth.

erated tail differs from the original in both shape and color. Most often the regenerated tail is turnip-shaped or bulbous, has an irregular scalation, and is of a paler color than the original.

The adult pattern of leopardlike dark spots usually stands out in bold relief against the paler ground color. The markings are often best defined on the dorsal surface of the head and on the tail.

The young are strongly cross-banded with dark brown against a ground color of yellow. The dark bands diffuse with the gecko's growth and age, and the yellow ground color often pales to a straw color. Some adults retain at least vestiges of the juvenile banding throughout their lives.

Leopard geckos are now readily available (albeit, sometimes expensive) in numerous genetically determined designer colors and patterns. Among others are
• High Yellow: Similar to the "normal" leopard geckos, but with brighter yellow ground coloration and often a reduction in dark spotting.
• Hyperxanthic: This phase is a "high yellow, high yellow"—in other words, these geckos are clad in a ground color of bright yellow and

This is a normally colored leopard gecko.

have a reduced dark pattern. This phase is marketed by some breeders as the "ghost leopard gecko."
• Tangerine: The common name describes this phase perfectly.
• Pastels: Again, the hobbyist-coined name is descriptive. Both the ground color and the highlights are muted. Head and tail patterns are standard.
• Lavender: Rather than being narrow, or reduced, and brown, the dark bands and spots of this morph are broad, prominent, and of a purplish hue.
• Striped: This morph has a broad, light middorsal stripe that is usually prominently margined with dark pigment. Lateral striping may also be present. Even the tail bears a vertebral stripe, but this is often uneven and may be less well defined than the trunk stripe. The ground color can be yellow or tangerine.

• Snow: This gecko has the yellow or orange ground color replaced by white(ish). There are black highlights. The lightest individuals (those with the fewest black markings) are considered the most desirable.
• Jungle: This pattern morph has a busy pattern of stripes and bands.
• Leucistic: Leucistic leopard geckos are a pale yellow to an off-white, have an ash-gray, unmarked tail, and an ash-gray head that usually lacks most markings including the bridle. There are usually traces of darker markings on the trunk, and the tubercles are grayish white.
• Albino: Rather than being white, this interesting phase has discernible, but muted, colors, but it does have the requisite pink eyes. Albinism has now been bred into many color morphs of this lizard.
• Blizzard: Pure white.

Hobbyists now breed leopard geckos for more and brighter yellows and oranges.

Leopard geckos are capable of vocalizing. Their repertoire of squeaks or clicks is most often voiced by sparring males.

Size and Lifespan

This gecko is fully grown at between 7 and 12 inches (18–30 cm) in total length. This is a long-lived gecko, 15 to 22 years not being an uncommon age among well-cared-for captives.

Natural Range

This is a gecko of rocky aridland habitats of Pakistan and India. It is a nocturnal, terrestrial species.

Captive Care

Since leopard geckos are not overly active, their terraria can be relatively small. Although we prefer to provide them large quarters, a terrarium made from a 10-gallon (37.8-L)

tank is sufficiently large for one male and one or two females. Plastic sweater or blanket boxes are also perfectly adequate. Because adult males are very territorial, more than one male should not be kept in a single cage.

The substrate in your leopard gecko terrarium may consist of an inch or two (2.5–5.1 cm) of sand, small pebbles, cypress mulch, calci-sand, or other such material. Several corkbark hides or plastic hideboxes should be provided for your geckos. Hollow cholla (*Cylindropuntia*) skeletons also provide excellent hiding areas and visual barriers. If you choose to include desert plants—succulents such as any of several varieties of low-growing *Sanseveria* and *Haworthia* are excellent choices—the terrarium will need to be well lit during the hours of daylight.

Leucistic leopard geckos are now firmly established in the hobby.

The plants may be planted directly into the terrarium substrate, but we have found that leaving them in their pots and sinking the pot into the terrarium substrate is easier, often better, for the plant and will allow you to easily switch the plants out if it becomes necessary. Fluorescent "plant-grow" bulbs are better for your plants than cool white or other more normally used household bulbs. Also, fluorescent bulbs emit less heat than incandescent bulbs. Desert plants must be watered, but usually only sparingly. Overwatering can rot the crowns and stems, but underwatering can be nearly as bad. As always, experience will be the best teacher.

Although the plants will need light, the geckos, nocturnal themselves, will not.

Cage furniture must be securely fastened to, or sitting on, the terrarium bottom glass. If furniture merely rests on the top of the sand, your gecko may dig beneath it, causing the article to shift, resulting in injury to the lizard.

Breeding

Without question, the leopard gecko is now the most commonly bred lizard in the United States, and among the most popular in Europe and Asia as well.

Adult male leopard geckos have larger preanal pores than the females and a more bulbous postanal area. The geckos should be cooled for about 60 days during the winter. A cagefloor temperature of 65°F (18°C) at night and 72°F (22°C) during the day will usually suffice. At that time, photoperiod should also be reduced. This is a period of reduced activity and feeding, not a period of hibernation.

After a period of two months, warm the geckos and begin feeding them heavily again. Offer them crickets, mealworms, and other insects, as well as a rather high percentage of newly born (pinky) mice. A female leopard gecko can produce four to seven clutches of two eggs each during each breeding season. They will usually readily accept a receptacle containing an inch or so (2.5 cm) of barely moistened sand-peat mixture for egg laying. It is best to move the eggs to an incubator preset at a temperature of 84 to 87°F (29–30.5°C) the morning after they are laid.

It is important that the moisture content of the incubation medium is neither too dry nor too wet, or the eggs will either desiccate or overhydrate. A mixture of six parts vermiculite to four parts of water (by volume) will provide the proper moisture content in the medium. You may choose to also place a shallow dish of water on top of the vermiculite to assure a relative humidity close to 100 percent is constantly maintained. The eggs should be laid on their sides on top of the vermiculite or be buried about halfway in a shallow depression. It is best if the eggs are not rotated on their longitudinal axes when they are being moved.

Because leopard geckos are among the reptiles with temperature-dependent sex determination (TDSD), the incubation temperature during the first trimester will determine the sex of the embryos. The suggested temperature of 84 to 87°F (29–30.5°C) will produce both sexes. Cooler temperatures will produce mostly females and warmer temperatures will produce males. Although embryo mortality is usually high, those eggs that survive temperatures above 90°F (32°C) will produce, not males, but large, robust, aggressive "superfemales."

Other Geckos with Similar Needs

Many relatives of the leopard gecko, including the banded geckos (*Coleonyx* sp.) of the southwestern United States, Mexico, and northern Central America, will thrive as captives under the terrarium conditions described under this heading. Other less frequently seen species, such as helmeted geckos (*Gekkonia*), the various knob-tailed geckos (*Nephrurus*), and the Namib gecko (*Chondrodactylus*), are also candidates for the aridland terrarium.

Fat-tailed Gecko

Hemitheconyx caudicinctus

Description

The beautiful fat-tailed gecko has vertically elliptical pupils and functional eyelids, and lacks the expanded digital discs that are so typical of most true geckos. They are heavy bodied, big headed, and short-legged. There are essentially two pattern morphs of the fat-tailed gecko—the banded and the striped. Both are banded with dark brown against a ground color of tan or buff (other adult colorations vary from a ground color of rosy tan, tan, pinkish tan, or orangish tan, to khaki). The tail is also banded and the original tail is strongly annulated. The striped morph has a narrow to wide white vertebral stripe.

The most spectacular of the designer morphs is the leucistic phase. This has a ground color of creamy yellow with cross bands of almost pure white.

When nervous or hunting, fat-tails elevate their tail and wag it sinuously. A fat-tailed gecko easily autotomizes (breaks) its tail; therefore, it should never be lifted by the tail.

Male fat-tailed geckos squeak and "click" when upset or involved in territorial disputes.

Although still expensive, albino fat-tailed geckos are readily available.

Size and Lifespan

Fully adult males attain an overall length of more than 8 inches (20 cm). A large, well-nourished (but not obese) male may have a tail more than 1¼ inches (3.8 cm) wide at the thickest point. Females are somewhat smaller. Longevity of more than 10 years is not uncommon.

Natural Range

This gecko is the tropical West African equivalent of the Asian leopard gecko. It occurs in dry, rocky woodlands and savannas and their environs. A secretive terrestrial gecko that secludes itself beneath debris or in the untenanted burrows of other small animals, it is thought to be largely inactive during the driest times of the year.

Captive Care

Once acclimated, fat-tailed geckos are very hardy. Imported specimens may prove difficult to successfully acclimate and even after successful acclimatization, have often proven difficult to breed. For these reasons we urge you to acquire only captive-bred/captive-hatched specimens.

Captive fat-tailed geckos quiet quickly and may become accus-

A normal fat-tailed gecko adult.

tomed to gentle handling. The best method for lifting your fat-tailed gecko is to shoo it into a can or some other receptacle from which it is unable to scramble or jump. Should that not be possible, cup the gecko gently in your hands; if it jumps or falls it may injure itself.

Adult male fat-tailed geckos are not compatible with other adult males. They may be kept singly or in small groups of one male and two females. An enclosure for a trio should have 12 × 24 inches (30 × 61 cm) or more of floor space. A secure hiding area should be provided for each lizard. The cage substrate should be of bark nuggets and the cage humidity should be reasonably high. If humidity is too low, the fat-tailed gecko(s) may have difficulty shedding. Cage humidity can be elevated by increasing the size of the water dish or by growing live plants (such as *Sanseveria* or *Haworthia*) in the terrarium.

Fat-tail geckos drink readily from low water dishes and avidly accept most types of insects and newly born mice as prey.

Breeding

Sexing mature fat-tailed geckos is a rather simple matter. The preanal pores are better developed on male fat-tailed geckos than on females. Because of the hemipenial bulges, the postanal area of the male is also more bulbous.

To breed successfully your fat-tails should be in topnotch condition. About 60 days of winter cooling (65°F at night and 72°F [18–22°C] during the day) will stimulate the reproductive cycle. A reduced photoperiod during the cooling is beneficial. This is not a period of hibernation.

Following the designated period of cooling, warm the geckos and feed them heavily. Offer them crickets, mealworms, and other insects, as well as a rather high percentage of newly born (pinky) mice. A female fat-tailed gecko can produce four to seven clutches of two eggs each during each breeding season.

A brightly colored adult striped fat-tailed gecko.

Fill a laying receptacle with a barely moistened sand-peat mixture about an inch (2.5 cm) in depth. It is best to remove the eggs and place them in an incubator the morning after they are laid.

The soft-shelled eggs of the fat-tailed gecko are not difficult to hatch, but it is important that the moisture content of the incubation medium is neither too dry nor too wet, or the eggs will either desiccate or overhydrate. A mixture of six parts vermiculite to four parts of water will provide the proper moisture content in the medium. You may choose to also place a shallow dish of water on top of the vermiculite to assure that a relative humidity close to 100 percent is constantly maintained. The eggs should be laid on their sides on top of the vermiculite or be buried about halfway in a shallow depression. It is best if the eggs are not rotated on their longitudinal axes when they are being moved.

The incubation temperature during the first trimester will determine the sex of a fat-tailed gecko. To produce both sexes, keep the incubation temperature between 84 and 87°F (29–30.5°C). Temperatures below 83°F (28°C) will produce mostly females. If embryo death does not occur, temperatures of 80°F (26.8°C) or below will produce all females. If the nest temperature is 88 to 90°F (31.1–32.2°C), male fat-tails will develop. Although embryo mortality is usually high, those eggs that survive temperatures above 90°F (32.2°C) will produce not males, but large, robust, aggressive "superfemales."

Other Geckos with Similar Needs

A great many other tropical geckos may be kept under the conditions described under this heading. Among these are bow-fingered geckos (*Cyrtodactylus*), ocelot geckos (*Paroedura*), and others.

Crested Gecko

Rhacodactylus ciliatus

Description

The common name is derived from the crests of elongated scales that begin over each eye, parallel the outline of the head, and continue down the back. They terminate at the base of the tail. Similarly, the scientific name of *ciliatus* refers to these ciliate scales.

Although it is quietly attractive, despite being given colorful (even fanciful) names by hobbyist breeders, the crested gecko is not brightly colored. The ground color varies from tan to brown to terra-cotta. There are often darker (or more rarely, lighter) spots on the back. The dark-spotted form is referred to by hobbyists as the "Dalmatian morph." The sides may be darker or brighter than the back. A light spot is present at the base of the tail on the dorsal surface, and may extend along the entire upper surface of the tail. Color changes are quite normal but also quite limited. The same crested gecko is very apt to be much darker at night than during the hours of daylight. The tail is quite prehensile and is bluntly rounded at the tip. The undersurface of the tail is flattened and bears "anti-skid"

The penny shows the comparative size of an hour-old crested gecko.

lamellae similar to those under the broadly flattened toes.

Size and Lifespan

This gecko attains a length of about 8 inches (20 cm). Its slender tail is somewhat less than half of the total length. A lifespan of from five to fifteen years may be expected.

Natural Range

Like others of this genus, the crested gecko is restricted in distribution to New Caledonia and nearby islands. Initially, this gecko was thought to be rare, then after years passed without any actual sightings, it was thought to be extinct. It actually is extant and well. It is arboreal, but seems to prefer shrubs and small trees.

Captive Care

This is an omnivorous gecko. It not only eats a variety of insect prey, but it avidly consumes a liquefied fruit mixture as well. Be sure that the crickets or other insects are dusted weekly with a good vitamin D_3-calcium additive. Gravid females and fast-growing babies should be provided calcium additives twice weekly.

Although usually a slow-moving species, if frightened, this gecko is

This crested gecko is cleaning his brille (the eye covering).

capable of bursts of quite considerable speed. Handle it carefully, grasping it gently but firmly to prevent excess squirming or escape. It can be injured if dropped. Avoid grasping it by the tail as this gecko autotomizes (loses) its tail easily. Once the tail is lost, this species seldom regenerates it.

This gecko prefers a humid, but not saturated, atmosphere.

Although this is an arboreal gecko that will use the upper part of a vertically oriented enclosure, such cage orientation is not mandatory. In fact, many keepers maintain a pair or a trio (one male and two females) in a normally oriented 10-gallon (37.8-L) terrarium. The cage should be provided with diagonal or horizontal limbs (perches) that are at least one and a half times the diameter of the gecko's body. The geckos will use the horizontal perches most readily if they are situated near the top of the terrarium. Crested geckos should be

encouraged to use the perches and discouraged from clinging vertically to the terrarium side. Although apparently a natural position in the wild, in captivity even those crested geckos being provided ample calcium additives may develop a malady known as "floppy tail syndrome." Although the geckos so affected look normal when in a diagonal or horizontal position, when perched head down, the tail flops upward at the base. There is no known cure for this problem.

The addition of live vining plants such as *Epipremnum aureum* ("pothos") will not only provide visual barriers and security, but will also add humidity to the terrarium.

Breeding
In only a decade, the crested gecko has emerged from comparative obscurity to a position of hobby favorite. During this remarkable transition they have also gone from

> **FRUIT-HONEY MIXTURE FORMULA FOR CRESTED GECKOS AND OTHERS**
>
> 1 tablespoon of pureed apricot, papaya, banana, or mixed baby food
> 1 teaspoon of honey
> 4 drops of Avitron liquid bird vitamins
> Pinch of vitamin D_3-calcium powder (such as Miner-all)
> ¼ teaspoon of bee pollen (optional)
> Just enough water to make this a soupy consistency
>
> Feed daily. Refrigerate unused portion. Discard any not used in one week.

being one of the most expensive of lizards to being easily affordable. Fortunately, they have proven to be an easy species to breed in captivity. Adults are easily sexed. The males have enlarged hemipenial bulges and prominent femoral pores. Crested geckos are prolific. Females have been known to produce up to nine clutches of two eggs each in a single breeding season. A slight winter cooling for a period of about 60 days is suggested, but may not be mandatory.

Gravid females should be provided with an egg-deposition box that contains an inch (2.5 cm) of moist (the keyword here is *moist*, not wet) laying medium. Either milled peat moss or sphagnum moss are good choices for this. The eggs should be left in place until the shells are dry. They should then be moved to an incubator. It is best if the eggs are not turned on their axis while being moved

The soft-shelled eggs should be incubated on a moist medium of vermiculite, perlite, or unmilled sphagnum. At a temperature between 77 and 81°F (25–27.2°C), the eggs will hatch in about two months. The babies will begin feeding on small crickets and fruit-honey mixture within two or three days. The crickets should be dusted with vitamin D_3-calcium additive at least twice weekly.

This is a fast-growing gecko. Maturity can be attained in under a year, and breeding may occur at about 12 months of age.

Other Geckos with Similar Needs

Day geckos (*Phelsuma* sp.) and other arboreal geckos of moderate size (flying geckos, *Ptychozoon*, house geckos, *Hemidactylus*, and wall geckos, *Tarentola*) all require captive conditions similar to the crested gecko. Day geckos are, of course, diurnal, while the others are nocturnal. The activity periods of the individual species must always be considered when feeding the lizards. Most anoles will also do well if provided these conditions.

Inland Bearded Dragon

Pogona vitticeps

Description

This is a spiny, heavy-bodied, lizard that has, over the years, become a hobbyist favorite. The common name of "bearded dragon" is derived from the darkened, distensible throat of the male. Males display the throat prominently during territoriality disputes. They were once available only in what has come to be called a normal (or wild) coloration. Originally intended to describe the dragons having a ground color of tan, brownish, grayish, or, more rarely, olive green, we now know that "normal" is an almost meaningless designation, for the ground color of inland bearded dragons in the wild varies well beyond these colors. In fact, the ground color of the inland dragon usually closely matches the substrate on which it is found: Those on dark soils are dark, those on light soils are light, and those from the red soil interior of Australia are reddish. On all, the face is banded and lighter dorsolateral markings are present. The markings are best defined on the juveniles and females, but fade on old males, and colors are most intense when the

The common name of the bearded dragon is derived from the distensible dark gular area.

lizard is hot and active. Through selective breeding, hobbyists have further enhanced the lighter and brighter colors. One of the more beautiful color morphs has come to be known as the **sandfire dragon**. As might be expected, the cost of inland bearded dragons is dependent on the color, with the normal colors being the least expensive. Let's take a quick look at some of the colors now available.

• The two most sought-after red dragons would seem to be the sandfire morph and the red flame morph. Sandfires tend to have a muted pattern and may be goldish orange, orange, or orange-red. Against this brilliance, the black beard of a breeding male is particularly evident. Females are brilliantly colored but have a more prominent pattern than adult males. The red flame morph is more strongly patterned than the sandfire. Facial markings are prominent. The ground color is orangish tan to buff and the dorsolateral blotches are a more brilliant orange to orange-red. The area at the angle of the jaws is often brilliant orange.

• The black tiger morph has a yellowish to orange body and broad, very dark, strongly contrasting lateral bands. The names of golden-

Provided their quarters are hot and dry, inland bearded dragons are one of the most easily kept lizard species.

headed and red-headed are self-descriptive. Both of these morphs have a head that is more brightly colored than their body. The pastel dragon has an orange-red head but is otherwise a grayish blue or grayish pink, almost opalescent, hue.

• Although it is not brightly colored, the German giant morph of the inland bearded dragon is impressive because of its size. It is a large, heavy-bodied, grayish dragon that is probably a hybrid between the eastern and the inland dragons.

Male dragons are often more colorful than females, but even the brightest of dragons are very dark when cold.

Hatchlings of all of the color phases mentioned are very similar and do not begin to brighten until they are about one-third grown.

Size and Lifespan

Males attain an adult length of 16 to 22 inches (40.6–55.8 cm). Females are usually smaller. A longevity of eight to ten years may be attained.

Natural Range

Dry savanna and aridland regions in eastern Australia. It is replaced in coastal areas by the eastern bearded dragon, *P. barbatus*.

Captive Care

Providing it is kept hot and dry, the inland bearded dragon is very easily kept. Inland bearded dragons

Capabale of metachrosis, inland beared dragons are lightest and brightest when suitably hot and content, and darkest when cold or stressed.

are now bred annually by the thousands and have an immense and devoted following in the United States. Tailor the food insects to the size of the dragons, always keeping the insects proportionately small. Full-spectrum lighting should be provided. The temperature on the surface of the basking spot should be 110–125°F (43.3–51.6°C). A thermal gradient is necessary.

Although they can move quickly when it is necessary, inland bearded dragons are usually quite "laid back" in attitude. Bearded dragons will thrive in a cage of moderate size. From one to several babies may be "started" in a 10- to 15-gallon (37.8–56.7-L) capacity container, but the lizards grow quickly and will soon need a larger cage. We suggest a cage having a floor space of no less than 18 × 36 inches (46 × 94 cm) (larger is better) for one or two dragons, and of no less than 18 × 48 inches (46 × 122 cm) for a trio of the lizards (again, larger is better). Visual barriers and hideboxes will be utilized.

Bearded dragons are prone to calcium metabolism disorders. Be certain that the calcium/phosphorus ratios are at least 2:1 in favor of calcium and that sufficient D_3 is provided to permit calcium metabolism. This is particularly important to fast-growing baby dragons and to ovulating females.

The diet of the inland bearded dragon should consist of both vegetation and insects. Babies tend to be

When attempting to warm up, inland bearded dragons flatten and tilt their bodies toward the sun.

more insectivorous than the adults. A mixture of very finely chopped greens (collards, turnip, nasturtium, dandelion), dandelion and hibiscus blossoms, squash, apples, and berries provides an excellent cross section of vegetation (avoid spinach, a calcium binder), and king mealworms, crickets, roaches, and waxworms are all easily procured insects. Care should be taken to feed *only* proportionately small crickets to these lizards. Large insects, if swallowed whole, as dragons are wont to do, may cause tetanic seizures that can result in the death of the lizard.

Adult male bearded dragons are very aggressive toward each other and cannot be kept together. If adult males are able to see each other, it is sometimes not possible to keep them in different cages in the same room. Providing they are not crowded, one male and one, two, or three females are usually compatible. Dragons can climb, but are primarily terrestrial. Cover the cage.

The cage should be well ventilated and the cage humidity should be low. A very hot basking spot, preferably illuminated with full-spectrum lighting, is needed, but the cage must be large enough and provide a sufficient thermal gradient for the dragon to cool when needed. A hotspot temperature of 110 to 120°F (43.3–48.9°C) (a little hotter is acceptable) will allow the lizards to quickly elevate their body temperature to optimum temperature. It is then that all bodily functions, from territoriality to foraging to digestion to reproductive behavior, are most efficient.

Breeding

Some degree of cycling is often necessary to breed bearded dragons successfully. Maintain a natural photoperiod throughout the year. This can be accomplished by manually turning the lights on and off, or by having the cage lighting controlled by a photocell.

During the winter months (late November through mid-February) the cage temperature should also be reduced somewhat. Reduce the temperature of the basking spot to about 85°F (29.4°C); this can be done by reducing the size of the bulb or by altering the distance of the bulb from the sand.

The appetite of your dragon may be curtailed somewhat by the cooler temperatures. Adjust accordingly.

In late February, increase the cage temperatures again. This can be done over a period of a week or so, or all at once. Your dragon's appetite will increase once more. Feed it heavily. Provide calcium supplements.

Your female will dig a nest several inches deep with her forefeet in barely moistened sand. After determining that the nest is suitable, she will reverse her position and lay her clutch, often with just her nose visible.

Young sexually mature inland dragon females can be amazingly prolific. Large, well-fed females may produce more than 150 eggs a year (occasionally with more than 35 in a clutch). Fecundity decreases after the lizards attain four or five years of age, and egg laying may cease at six or seven years of age.

The eggs should be incubated in a barely damp medium at a temperature of from 80 to 85°F (26.7–29.4°C); 82–83°F (27.8–28°C) is optimal. Incubation will take 72 to 85 days.

Hatchlings require hot temperatures and frequent feeding. The insects offered should be proportionately small. Hungry hatchlings may squabble and even bite each other. Provide them with food once or twice daily.

Other Lizards with Similar Needs

Other species of bearded dragons will thrive as captives with the regimen of care provided for the inland bearded dragon, as will desert iguanas, *Dipsosaurus dorsalis*, and chuckwallas, *Sauromalus ater*.

Australian (Eastern) Blue-tongued Skink

Tiliqua scincoides scincoides

Description

This short-legged, long-bodied skink has a grayish, tan, or olive brown ground color and broad cross bands of darker olive, charcoal, brown, or reddish brown. Some individuals have pinkish blotches on the sides. The scales are not keeled. The head is broadened posteriorly. There is a prominent dark postocular stripe behind each eye and a black spot may be present on each side of the neck.

Size and Lifespan

This is a large, heavy-bodied skink. An adult size of 17 inches (43 cm) is occasionally attained, but most examples are an inch or two (2.5 cm) smaller. Captives have lived for 20+ years.

Natural Range

This is a skink of habitats that vary from grasslands to woodlands, but it is not associated with arid-lands. It is found throughout much of southern and eastern Australia.

Occasional albino northern blue-tongued skinks are found, but designer colors have not yet been stabilized by hobbyists.

Captive Care

Providing their terrarium is kept warm and humid, the eastern blue-tongued skink is an easily kept lizard. Many are now bred annually by hobbyists, and blue-tongues have become a popular pet lizard. Full-spectrum lighting should be provided. The temperature on the surface of the basking spot should be 90 to 100°F (32.2–37.8°C). A thermal gradient should always be provided.

When they are trying to move quickly, blue-tongued skinks fold their legs against their body and move away in an undulatory serpentine motion. When unhurried, they simply walk on all four of their short legs and drag the belly along the ground surface. Eastern blue-tongues may hiss, loll their cobalt blue tongue out, or even bite if frightened, but most examples tame quickly. These skinks will thrive in a cage of moderate size. From one to several babies may be "started" in a 10- to 15-gallon (37.8–56.7-L) capacity container, but the lizards grow quickly and will soon need a larger cage. We suggest a cage having a floor space of no less than

Although a few are still imported from New Guinea, most blue-tongued skinks in the American pet market are now captive-bred.

18 × 36 inches (46 × 94 cm) (larger is better) for one or two adult blue-tongues and of no less than 18 × 48 inches (46 × 122 cm) for a trio of the lizards (again, larger is better). Visual barriers and hideboxes should be provided.

Rapidly growing blue-tongued skinks are very susceptible to calcium metabolism disorders. Be certain that calcium supplements are provided, that the calcium/phosphorus ratios are at least 2:1 in favor of calcium, and that sufficient vitamin D_3 is provided to permit calcium metabolism. This is particularly important to fast-growing baby skinks and to ovulating females.

A hot basking spot, preferably illuminated with full-spectrum lighting, is needed, but the cage must be large enough and provide a sufficient thermal gradient for the dragon to cool when it chooses. The hotspot is of particular importance to gravid

females. A temperature of about 100°F (37.8°C) will allow the lizards to quickly elevate their body temperature to optimum temperature and to thermoregulate throughout the day.

The diet of the inland bearded dragon should consist of both vegetation and meat. Babies tend to be less interested in the vegetable matter than the adults. Canned cat or dog foods, crickets, and king mealworms will provide the animal protein for the skinks. The lizards will also eat diced apples, peaches, bananas, mangos, papayas, and other fruits. You can also offer them very finely chopped greens (collards, turnip, nasturtium, dandelion), dandelion and hibiscus blossoms, squash, apples, and berries (avoid spinach, a calcium binder).

Adult male blue-tongues are very aggressive toward each other and cannot be kept together. Gravid females are also aggressive and if kept colonially, must be watched carefully. Providing they are not crowded, one male and one, two, or three females are usually compatible. These skinks are terrestrial.

Breeding

Some degree of cycling is often necessary to breed blue-tongued skinks successfully. Maintain a natural photoperiod throughout the year. This can be accomplished by manually turning the lights on and off, or by having the cage lighting controlled by a photocell.

During the winter months (late November through mid-February) the cage temperature should also be reduced somewhat. Reduce the temperature of the basking spot to about 85°F (29.4°C); this can be done by reducing the size of the bulb or by altering the distance the bulb is from the sand.

The appetite of your skinks may diminish somewhat while they are being cooled.

In late February, increase the cage temperatures again. This can be done over a period of a week or so, or all at once. Your skinks' appetite will increase again. Feed them heavily. Provide calcium supplements.

Adult female eastern blue-tongued skinks may give birth to up to 25 babies. They will breed annually for many years.

Neonates require warmth, frequent feeding, and daily calcium supple-ments. Hungry babies may bite each other, but eastern blue-tongues are less apt to do this than more aggressive species of blue-tongued skinks.

Other Lizards with Similar Needs

Except for the blotched blue-tongued skink, *Tiliqua nigrolutea*, which is also of rather benign disposition, other blue-tongues are often quarrelsome among themselves. Once the compatibility problem is addressed, however, other species of blue-tongued skinks will thrive as captives with the regimen of care provided for the eastern form. So, too, will many of the larger American skinks such as Great Plains, *Eumeces obsoletus*, and broad-headed, *Eumeces laticeps*.

The tip of the namesake blue tongue can be seen here.

Red-footed Tortoise
Chelonoidis carbonaria

Description

Red-footed tortoises are the predominant tortoise species in the American pet trade. There are many designations—"dwarf cherry head" and "Bolivian giant," among them—which are actually quite misleading. For example, the dwarf cherry heads do have brightly colored heads, but they are not dwarfs. And the so-called Bolivian giants probably originate elsewhere. But one thing is for sure—they are red-foots.

The red-footed tortoise has a long, rather narrow, and highly domed carapace. Many examples from Colombia actually have a dumbbell shape when viewed from above. Normally the carapace is dark with light centers in each scute and light spots along the edges of the marginals. The scales on the forelimbs vary from a rather pale yellowish orange to a bright reddish orange, and the larger plates on the head are equally variable. The marginals do not have strongly serrate edges. The plastron may vary from predominantly yellow with a black center to exactly the opposite, black with a yellow center.

This 14-inch-long (35-cm), typically colored adult red-foot has been captive for more than 20 years.

Size and Lifespan

Geographically variable in size, some adults are fully grown at 10 inches (25 cm) in shell length while others may attain 18 inches (46 cm). Fortunately, most red-footed tortoises now available in the American pet industry, top out at 12 to 13 inches (30–33 cm) in shell length. The longevity of the red-footed tortoise should be well in excess of 30 years.

Natural Range

This beautiful tortoise ranges widely from southernmost Panama southward to Argentina. However, it is absent from most of the northern and central Amazon drainages. It occurs east of the Andes. It has also been introduced to some West Indian Islands, including Trinidad and Barbados. It is a species of thornscrub habitats and sparsely vegetated savannas.

Captive Care

These tortoises are wonderfully hardy, prettily colored, personable, small enough to be easily maintained, and affordable. In today's world of pets, this is an unusual suite of positives.

Hatchling red-foots are often available in pet stores and at "herp expos." They are a tropical species

This is a several-week-old red-footed tortoise.

from high-humidity habitats, so temperature and cage humidity will require addressing. Acceptable cage size will, of course, depend on the size and number of tortoises being kept.

When content, red-foots are wanderers. Although two or three hatchlings can be housed nicely in a 20-gallon (75.7-L) long terrarium (12 × 12 × 30 inches [30 × 30 × 76 cm]), one or two adults should be provided, when possible, with a 6 × 12-foot (1.8 × 3.65-m) (or larger) naturalistic enclosure. This can be easily made from pieces of lumber if a backyard is available. It will need to be about 20 inches (51 cm) in height. In the southern United States, red-foots can be kept outdoors in a setup such as this for six months or more of the year, especially if artificial heat is provided. In the North, temperatures

suitable to a red-foot's outdoor life may occur for only two or three summer months. Apartment and condo dwellers do not have this caging latitude. They will have to provide the largest cage possible in an indoor setting. A cage of 4 × 8 feet (1.2 × 2.4 m)—the size of a sheet of plywood—will suffice, if available. If the cage must be smaller, the tortoise should be allowed to frequently exercise in a warm room (the floor temperature must be considered also!). Use nonskid flooring. Intermediate-sized red-foots can be provided with intermediate-sized caging. A hidebox large enough for all tortoises to gather in should be provided.

When kept outside and fed a healthy diet, natural sunlight should allow the tortoise to produce and metabolize all of the calcium needed. However, when indoors, vitamin D_3

Orange carapacial areolae (scute centers) are normally well developed.

and calcium additives should be added to the diet, even if a full-spectrum basking bulb is provided.

Offer your red-foot a diet that consists primarily of vegetable matter. Among other things, a mixture of collard greens, romaine, grated carrots, apples, a few tomatoes, turnip greens, green beans, yellow squash, zucchini, and okra can be given. Sprinkle these once weekly (thrice weekly for fast-growing hatchlings or ovulating females) with a D_3-calcium powder. Provide fresh water in a low bowl into which your tortoise can climb to sit and soak its feet and plastron for a while. The water should be changed as needed, but at least once every three days.

Breeding

Adult female red-foots have a flat plastron (lower shell) and a short tail. The plastron of an adult male is concave and the tail is large. Tortoise breeding is a lengthy affair. Males indulge in a prolonged courtship that includes bobbing and nodding of his head, circling the female, nipping at her shell and face to immobilize her, and, finally, mounting and breeding. While mounted (and sometimes during courtship) the male will utter a series of clucks and wheezes.

Like most tortoises, red-foots dig a nest in yielding soil for their eggs. The digging of the nest is accomplished by the female with her hind feet. Each clutch can contain between one and twelve eggs. Several clutches can be produced each season at intervals of about 30 days. At 82 to 86°F (27.8–30°C), incubation can take from three and a half to six months. Hatchlings are about 1½ inches (4.6 cm) in length.

Occasional red-foots have light radiations on the carapace.

Other Tortoises and Turtles with Similar Needs

The yellow-footed tortoise, *Chelonoidis denticulata*, of South America is the rain forest equivalent of the savanna-dwelling red-foot. The yellow-foot has a more rounded carapace (when viewed from above) and strongly serrate marginal scutes. The highly domed Asian elongated tortoise, *Geochelone elongata*, attains a length of about a foot (30 cm). It varies from an unrelieved tan to tan with variable black markings. It is a hardy and responsive species.

The following three species, the Hermann's tortoise, the wood turtle, and the eastern box turtle, can be hibernated during the winter months if you choose to do so. All are popular pets but availability varies.

Hermann's tortoise, *Testudo h. hermanni*, is a rather small European species. It is adult at 8 inches (20 cm) or less, and captive-hatched babies are often available. The highly domed carapace is black and tan in color. Except for preferring less humidity than the red-footed tortoise, the Hermann's tortoise will do well when caged and fed similarly.

• The North American wood turtle, *Glyptemys insculpta*, is less highly domed than true tortoises and box turtles.

• The wood turtle is brown dorsally and has yellow to orange highlights on the neck and limbs. This 10-inch-long (25-cm) turtle is now protected throughout its range in the northeastern United States, but captive-bred babies are often available.

Often referred to as Paraguayan dwarf cherry-headed red-footed tortoises, these tortoises are neither dwarfed nor from Paraguay.

Cherry-headed red-footed tortoises, a coveted form, are now being captive bred in some numbers.

Check your laws before acquiring this species.

• The colorful eastern box turtle, *Terrapene c. carolina*, of the eastern United States is adult at only 7 inches (17.8 cm) in length. It has a hinged plastron. It is protected by law in many of the states in which it occurs and ownership may be restricted. Check your laws.

Razor-backed Musk Turtle

Sternotherus carinatus

Description

Although this is not a brightly colored turtle, it is small, quite inexpensive, and very hardy. Like all turtles, the razor-backed musk turtle can and will bite (painfully, if the turtle is more than 1½ inches [4.6 cm] in shell length) and if it is carelessly handled. Captive-hatched babies are seasonally available from some pet shops, but more routinely from on-line sources and at herp expos.

Hatchling razor-backed mud turtles are only about the size of a quarter. Dorsally, they are a warm gray to tan or olive brown in color and are patterned with darker streaks on the carapace and dark spots on the head. If viewed head on, the sides of the carapace will be seen to slope sharply and a prominent vertebral keel is present. The carapacial scutes overlap slightly. The posterior and lateral marginal scutes are strongly serrate. The plastron often has a pinkish tinge. Adults are similar in overall color, but are usually duller. The dark markings are less well defined and the marginal scutes are less serrate but the carapace remains razor-backed. Adult males

Adult male razor-backed musk turtles have large heads, strong jaws, and will bite if carelessly restrained.

have a very large head. The plastron is olive gray or olive brown in color.

Size and Lifespan

Although old adults may attain a carapace length of 6½ inches (16 cm), a length of between 4 and 5½ inches (10–14 cm) is more typical. Hatchlings are only about 1 inch (2.5 cm) in length. This turtle may live for more than 15 years.

Natural Range

This musk turtle ranges eastward from eastern Texas to Mississippi and northward to southeastern Oklahoma and southern Arkansas. It is common in river edge shallows, oxbows, and impoundments, and may be particularly abundant near fishing docks. It often basks on warm, sunny days.

Captive Care

The single thing that makes musk and mud turtles such excellent captives is their hardiness. Additionally, almost all are fairly small and they are not as dependent on full-spectrum lighting and basking as most other aquatic turtles.

From one to several hatchlings may be kept in an aquarium as small as 5 gallons (18.9 L) in capacity. The same number of half-grown musk

The common name of the razor-backed musk turtle is derived from the strongly defined carapacial keel.

turtles can be kept in a 15-gallon (56.7-L) tank. One, or a pair, of adults will thrive in a 20-gallon (75.7-L) long aquarium.

One very real fact is that large turtles will devastate a carefully planted and decorated aquarium. It is, therefore, better to keep tank furniture to a minimum and whatever is used functional and immovable. If the water is more than "neck deep," a ramp should be provided to allow the turtle to easily reach the surface. Secured formations of sloping smooth rock that the turtles can climb up easily are ideal and they are easily cleaned. A basking light can be placed above this, to warm the rock surface to about 90°F (32°C). The dry rock surface should be large enough to accommodate all of the turtles in the tank. Despite their small size, these turtles are quite strong. Their energetic dislodging of movable rocks and heaters with glass tubes has been known to break both the heater

and the aquarium glass. Unbreakable heaters and immovable rocks are both mandatory.

Razor-backed musk turtles also will thrive in garden fish ponds. However, they will easily catch and eat slow-moving fish such as goldfish so choose tankmates prudently. In the southern tier states (the Sunbelt), where freezes are unusual, the turtles can remain out year round. This holds true in other regions where the water temperature can be held at or above 68°F (20°C) with a tube heater. In my region of northcentral Florida, I depend on a 1000-watt, titanium (unbreakable), thermostatically controlled heater to keep the water temperature of the 250-gallon (945-L) pool at 68°F (20°C) or above throughout the winter.

Musk turtles are carnivorous. They will eat formulated turtle chow, minnows, tadpoles, worms, and insects.

The water provided should be free of chlorine and chloramines. It can

Baby razor-backed musk turtles have very strongly keeled shells with serrate marginal scutes.

be filtered (submergible powerheads on sponge filters are ideal) but will still require a weekly cleaning.

Breeding

Although wild-collected razor-backed musk turtles may require winter cooling to cycle them for breeding, captive-produced examples may not. It seems as if simply a natural photoperiod throughout the year will often suffice to stimulate the successful breeding of captive-produced musk turtles. When adult, musk turtles are easily sexed. A male has a long, thickened tail that ends in an enlarged horny plate, and widened areas of skin separate the plastral scutes. Females may be differentiated from the males by their tiny tail and the lack of skin between the plastral plates.

These turtles mate while submerged, usually on the bottom of their aquarium (or pond). The female leaves the water to dig the nest for her two to five eggs. Well-fed captive females may lay two clutches a year. At 78 to 82°F (26–28°C), incubation varies from 48 to 65 days. Once pipping the elongate eggs, the hatchlings may take up to three days longer to emerge.

Other Aquatic Turtles with Similar Needs

All other musk and mud turtles (*Sternotherus* and *Kinosternon*, respectively) will thrive if kept in the conditions outlined above. Most of these turtles are small but a few of the Latin American species may attain a shell length of 8 inches (20 cm) or slightly more, and the two species of giant musk turtles may attain a foot (30 cm) in length and may require a larger aquarium. Of all species, the red-cheeked mud turtle, *Kinosternon scorpioides cruentatum*, is the most colorful. Babies are especially so, having cheeks of medium to bright red. The juvenile colors usually dull with growth but some degree of red suffusion remains visible.

Ornate Horned Frog
Ceratophrys ornata

Description

This frog can and will bite—painfully! Handle it and work near it with care! The ornate horned frog is also known as the Argentine horned frog, but it is best known to thousands of hobbyists as the "Pac-Man frog." The name Pac-Man frog was coined because this frog's insatiable appetite seemed reminiscent of the interference gobbling, hero-icon of computer game fame. We simply refer to it as "the wonderful hopping mouth." This is a big-headed, strong-jawed, robust-bodied, short-legged frog. The ornate horned frog is patterned with various shades of green, terra-cotta, and peach, or a combination of these colors, against a lighter ground color. Yellows, blacks, and browns can also be incorporated into the color scheme. The horns are little more than nubbins. Males have a dark throat.

Albinos are now commonly seen, as are hybrids between the ornate and the Chaco horned frogs and the ornate and the Amazonian horned frogs.

Ornate horned frogs are known by hobbyists as "Pac-Man frogs."

Size and Lifespan

Females are the larger sex, and the largest females attain a length of 5 to 5½ inches (12.7–13.7 cm). Since they can be even broader than they are long—some of the largest females near salad-plate size—they are among the largest members of the genus. At a 2½- to 4½-inch (6- to 11-cm) length (again populational size differences apply), males are significantly smaller. Sexually mature males have a suffusion of dark pigment on the throat.

This horned frog may live for more than 15 years.

Natural Range

This species occurs in subtropical southern Brazil, contiguous Uruguay, and eastern-central Argentina.

Captive Care

The ornate horned frog will eat virtually anything that it was capable of overpowering, including live rodents, fish, insects, or worms. While eating, these frogs can often ingest fair amounts of their substrate, causing fatal intestinal impactions. To lessen the chance of impaction, feed your frog (every second day for fast-growing babies and once weekly for adults) with forceps or

A steady diet of pink mice is not healthy for horned frogs.

move the frog when feeding it to a receptacle having no substrate.

Because they are inactive, the ornate horned frog does not require a large terrarium. A 10-gallon (37.8-L) aquarium or a large-impact resistant plastic blanket box is sufficient for a single specimen. The frogs can be kept either in an inch (2.5 cm) or so of water or in a terrestrial setup. If you do opt for the water, remember to check the water cleanliness daily, or even twice daily. A frog this large can thoroughly foul its water in only a matter of minutes.

Many keepers simply slope a suitably sized receptacle containing nothing but a hiding cave and a little water in the low end.

If you choose to provide a substrate, several inches of moist, unmilled sphagnum moss is ideal. The frog will burrow down into the moss, usually keeping its head exposed, but being otherwise concealed. A shallow, easily cleaned water receptacle that is big enough for the frog to sit in can be sunk nearly to its rim in the moss. If the terrarium is large enough, a sturdy potted plant can be used to provide decoration and visual barriers.

The need for absolute terrarium cleanliness cannot be overemphasized.

Breeding

There are two methods of inducing horned frogs to breed. One is with the use of an injectable lutenizing and releasing hormone (LHRH—both sexes are stimulated by hormonal injection) and the second is termed natural cycling.

We prefer natural cycling over the hormonal stimulation.

Cool your horned frog (55–65°F [13–18°C]) for 30 to 45 days during the shortened days of winter. Simultaneously, reduce cage humidity (to simulate the dry season), if possible. Your horned frogs will become inac-

A capacious mouth and strong jaws make ornate horned frogs efficient predators.

tive and will conserve body moisture by forming a cocoon of several layers of loosened skin. After the cooling, increase both warmth and moisture and provide a large receptacle to simulate a seasonal pond. A plastic wading pool may be used for this. On a warm, muggy night, place your horned frogs in a pool containing 1½ to 2 inches (3.7–5.1 cm) of chlorine-chloramine free water. Using a recirculating pump and a sprayhead, spray the frogs for several hours a night and again during the day (you want to have the frogs think the rainy season is back!). Properly cycled males will begin calling. Breeding usually occurs from dusk through the early hours of darkness, and is usually terminated well before dawn.

Male horned frogs, ready to breed, undergo a few subtle changes in appearance. The males' throats darken somewhat and they will develop horny, black excrescences (projections) on the thumbs. These roughened pads help the male retain his grip during amplexus. The female will be clasped behind her forelimbs, usually while the pair is floating or sitting in shallow, quiet water. As the eggs are released, the male fertilizes them.

If possible, tape record the calls of the males, then use the tapes to

Nightcrawlers are usually eagerly accepted by horned frogs of all sizes.

stimulate the frogs. We suggest that the rain system be activated at least twice daily—once in the afternoon for an hour or an hour and a half, and again, beginning at late dusk, for from three to six hours.

Although it may take from two to four or five days, the "rain" should stimulate the breeding urges. Males will begin calling, swelling their dark throats and repeatedly producing a penetrating, metallic "whistle." (This phase of the breeding sequence may be hastened if you happen to have earlier made a tape recording of your horned frogs' breeding vocalizations and play it now.)

The males like to have all four feet firmly against the bottom of the tank while calling, so shallow water is imperative. The males may call each night for two or three nights before the females begin to respond. Once stimulated, females will begin approaching the chorusing males, or males may see a moving female and move to her to begin amplexus. If while searching for a female, a male grasps another male by accident, the grasped animal will produce vibrations and chirps to indicate the error. Unless the male is dislodged, amplexus may last for more than a day, but soon, following the initiation of amplexus, the male horned frog will begin periodically tapping the female's shoulder area with his bottom jaw. This apparently synchronizes ovulation and laying with sperm release, although sperm release may be instigated by the movement of the egg mass against the venter of the male.

The eggs are produced in gelatinous masses, and may number from only a few hundred to over 1,500.

The tadpoles grow quickly and are very cannibalistic. If not raised singly, even with adequate space, visual barriers, and ample food (worms and freshly killed fish), cannibalism is almost sure to occur.

Other Horned Frogs with Similar Needs

The Chacoan horned frog, *Ceratophrys cranwelli*, is another large species. It is usually of brown coloration. When the ornate and the Chacoan horned frogs are compared, the latter will be seen to have a proportionately larger head, longer horns, and squatter body than the ornate horned frog. This species ranges in suitable habitats from extreme southern Bolivia and Paraguay to central Argentina. Albinos are now readily available.

The Amazonian horned frog, *Ceratophrys cornuta*, is only sporadically available. It is smaller (to 3½ inches [19 cm]) and a more demanding captive than the ornate horned frog. The Amazonian horned frog is a tropical species and seems to prefer other frogs as prey. Be sure that any example in which you are interested is eating readily available food. This beautiful frog has long horns and may be brown-tan, reddish, green, or various combinations of these colors.

Oriental Fire-bellied Toad
Bombina orientalis

Description

The oriental fire-bellied toad is the only one of the several species that is readily available in the American pet marketplace. Dorsally it is lime to moss green with black mottling. The typical ventral color is bright red with black reticulations. However, captive-bred fire-bellies that are raised on a diet deficient in Beta-carotenes may have the red of the belly replaced by yellow or gray. The toetips are red (occasionally gray on captive-bred examples). This is a rather corpulent little toad with a warty skin. The eyes are prominent and are directed dorsolaterally, certainly an adaptation to enable this toad to more easily spy enemies approaching from above as it floats among the aquatic vegetation.

The vocal sac is internal. The calls are rapidly repeated, hollow-sounding hoots that are easily heard indoors, but have no great carrying power in the wild.

Size and Lifespan

Captive oriental fire-bellied toads have lived for more than 10 years. Both sexes attain an adult size of

The red venter of an oriental fire-bellied toad can vary in intensity and may occasionally be replaced by gray.

about 1¾ inches (4.4 cm). Females are of heavier build than the males.

Natural Range

This is a pretty little aquatic toad from Korea, China, and Manchuria. It inhabits the quiet, heavily vegetated waters of ditches, ponds, puddles, and backwaters. It can be very abundant in ideal habitats.

Captive Care

Oriental fire-bellied toads are very hardy and if kept clean and cool will live for many years in captivity. They are rather inactive but are almost always ready to eat. A 10-gallon (37.8-L) aquarium will house three or four adults nicely.

These toads may be kept in either an aquatic or a semiaquatic setup. If kept in an aquarium, the water must be clean and not contain chloramines or chlorine. A thick layer of floating plants (such as water sprite) or pieces of corkbark should be provided for the frogs to sit on. When kept in a semiaquatic terrarium, the frogs will often sit in the water right at the edge of the land area. Occasionally the opposite might occur. The land section may be formed of soil and covered with woodland mosses, or may simply be compacted, unmilled sphagnum moss.

Oriental fire-bellied toads are beautifully colored both above and below. They thrive in clean, filtered aquaria having ample floating cork, driftwood, or plant islands.

Hardy plants can be included in the setup, both to beautify the terrarium and to serve as visual barriers. Although fire-bellied toads are not particularly wary, visual barriers and hiding areas offer them security.

Daytime terrarium temperatures of 70–75°F (21–24°C) and nighttime lows of 65–68°F (18–20°C) are acceptable.

The skin secretions of fire-bellied toads are quite toxic. Be sure to wash your hands after handling these anurans. And just as a word of caution, it is very important that your hands be clean and that you are not wearing topical insect repellents, soap, chlorine, or sunscreen; these are very likely to kill the frog.

Because you are able to simply drop feed insects onto the land section of a semiaquatic terrarium, it is the easier of the two setups for the keeper. Feeding fire-bellied toads in an aquatic setup is more exacting and time-consuming. However, being able to see the beautiful undersides of fire-bellied toads as they lie quietly amid floating vegetation makes the aquatic setup well worth the extra effort needed to feed these frogs properly, in the estimation of many hobbyists. If the cover of floating plants is thick enough (or if corkbark is present), small crickets may be placed on these. However, since fire-bellies enjoy a varied diet, waxworms and small sections of earthworms can be impaled on a broom straw (take care that the end of the straw does not protrude) and presented to the floating toads. They will usually accept such offerings ravenously.

Breeding

When they are not in breeding condition, it is difficult to determine the sexes of oriental fire-bellied toads. However, females tend to be the more robust in build and to have narrower heads, factors that are not particularly helpful unless both sexes are present for comparison.

The pretty oriental fire-bellied toad is adult at only 2 inches (5 cm) in length.

When in breeding condition, males vocalize and develop horny grasping pads on the insides of their forelimbs and on the inner fingers.

To cycle fire-bellied toads successfully for breeding it will be necessary to provide both a natural photoperiod and to cool the frogs to about 60°F (15.5°C) for a period of 60 days. The toads will feed while cooled, but sparingly. After 60 days return your frogs to their natural regimen of warmth, feed them heavily, and put bunched plants such as *Anacharis* in the tank. Males will usually begin voicing their tooting calls after the tank is warmed again and breeding should ensue soon thereafter. A healthy female may lay from 40 to about 125 eggs, usually attaching them to submerged water plants. At a water temperature of 65 to 72°F (18–22°C) the eggs will hatch in three to seven days. The tadpoles will begin to show limited activity within two days post-hatch-

ing and after three or four days will begin foraging. They will eat infusoria and some tropical fish "fry" food. If conditions are optimum, metamorphosis will occur in three to four months.

The metamorphs will require vast quantities of tiny, vitamin-enhanced insects or other arthropods. Be certain that Beta-carotene is contained in the diet, or the toadlets will lack the traditional red-belly coloration. Termites, small crickets, sow bugs, flies, and the like will all be eagerly eaten.

Other Frogs with Similar Needs

The rice paddy frog, *Occidozyga lima*, will do well in either the semi-aquatic or the aquatic setup described above. Many other frogs and toads will thrive in the semi-aquatic setup but the size of the terrarium and the food offered may need to be tailored to species.

Dumpy Treefrog
Pelodryas caerulea

Description

This is a large, smooth-skinned, heavy-bodied treefrog. The color may vary from a very pretty jade green, to a rather bright green, to olive brown. Some examples have a bluish cast. This frog is also known as the "Australian green," "giant green," and "White's treefrog." The females of this species tend to develop heavy supratympanal folds that extend forward, and are best developed above the eyes. In some particularly old and obese specimens, these ridges may become so enlarged and pendulous that they actually droop over at least part of the eye, partially obscuring vision. Both sexes have a short, rounded nose.

It has been shown that the blue coloration of dumpy treefrogs may be caused by a diet deficient to a degree in Beta-carotene.

Some dumpy treefrogs have a variable amount of white spotting on their dorsum. Breeding programs are now underway to increase the amount of white present.

The glandular skin of the dumpy treefrog is resistant to desiccation. The belly skin is granular.

This feral dumpy treefrog was found in Lee County, Florida.

The toepads are large and although these frogs are proportionately stout, they climb well.

The territorial (and breeding) calls of White's treefrog are a single, harsh, often repeated croak.

Size and Lifespan

Male dumpy treefrogs seldom exceed 3½ inches (9 cm) in length, but some females may attain a length of almost 5 inches (13 cm).

White's treefrogs are very hardy and long-lived. Many captives have lived for more than 15 years, and it is probable that more than 25 years could be attained.

Natural Range

Dumpy treefrogs occur throughout the northern half of Australia and in southern New Guinea. Subtle morphological differences between the New Guinean and Australian populations indicate that they have long been discrete. Because they are resistant to desiccation and drought, dumpy treefrogs are able to colonize relatively dry regions. Examples from the southern part of the range have proven to be quite cold-tolerant. As would be expected, those from the more tropical areas of northern Australia and Indonesia are more cold-sensitive and

Dumpy treefrogs may change to brown from green.

must be kept warm throughout the year.

Captive Care

Dumpy treefrogs will thrive for years on a regimen of minimal care. They are quiet, are almost always ready to eat, and the somewhat comical appearance of old adults (especially old adult females) endears them to many folks who otherwise have little interest in frogs.

A 5-gallon (18.9-L) tank is large enough for two or three new metamorphs. A 10-gallon (37.8-L) tank will house two adults satisfactorily. In suitably warm weather dumpy treefrogs may be kept outside in cages of wood and wire construction (containing plants and a water dish). These frogs are particularly at home in heavily planted greenhouses.

Daytime terrarium temperatures of 80–85°F (26.8–29°C) and night-time lows of 68 to 75°F (20–24°C) are acceptable.

Because amphibians absorb moisture (and any impurities the moisture might contain) through their very permeable skin, when keeping amphibians, hygiene is an important issue. It is very important that your hands be clean and that you are not wearing topical insect repellents, soap, chlorine, or sunscreen.

The glandular secretions of a dumpy treefrog (and most other amphibian species) will irritate mucous membranes (eyes, nose, mouth, cuts, and abrasions). Wash your hands both before and after handling this frog species.

Breeding

Visual determination of the sex is difficult. Adult male dumpy treefrogs often develop a darker throat with "looser" skin than that of the female. The loose skin accommodates the swelling of the vocal sac during chorusing. Males are also slightly smaller than the females and when sitting quietly *may* do so with their forelimbs slightly less flexed than the females. When properly cycled prior to breeding, male dumpy treefrogs will also develop darkened, roughened nuptial (grasping) pads on the outsides of their thumbs.

To cycle healthy, heavy adults, provide a natural photoperiod and cool the frogs to about 68°F (20°C) for a period of 60 days. After 60 days return your frogs to their natural regimen of warmth and feed them heavily. After about a week, begin to use the hydration chamber. A healthy female may lay from 1,000 to 4,000 eggs. Decide on the number you wish to raise and discard the remainder. The "jelly-coated" eggs will hatch in three to seven days. The tadpoles will begin to show limited activity within two days post-hatching and after three or four days will begin foraging. They will scrape at trout chow, catfish chow, tropical fish "fry" food, and other such sources of animal protein. If conditions are optimum, metamorphosis may occur in just over four weeks' time, but can take up to two months and, rarely, a little longer.

At metamorphosis the mouth parts change from the tadpole's scraping, beaklike affair to the broad mouth of the adult. Changes occur in the gut, lungs replace gills, and the limbs, which have developed over a period of weeks, strengthen. Finally, the tail is absorbed, and the little frog leaves the water for a life on land.

The metamorphs require vast quantities of tiny, vitamin-enhanced insects or other arthropods.

Other Treefrogs with Similar Needs

The very large Indonesian White-lipped treefrog, *Litoria infrafrenata*, the equally large Cuban treefrog, *Osteopilus septentrionalis*, and several larger species of Asian flying frogs, *Rhacophorus* sp., may be kept using the parameters described above.

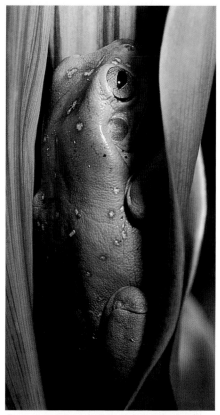

Dumpy treefrogs often hide by day but become active after dark.

Some dumpy treefrogs are liberally peppered with small, light spots.

Red-eyed Treefrog
Agalychnis callidryas

Description

Leaf frogs are a wonderfully adapted subgroup of neotropical hylid frogs. The generic name is pronounced *Ag-ah-lick-niss*.

The red-eyed treefrog has taken the pet industry by storm. Normally it has a green dorsum, but the shade of green is variable by temperature, other stresses, as well as by the frog's activity level. The dorsal color may be a dull olive green when the treefrog is cold or dry. A dark forest green may be assumed when the frog is resting, or if climatic conditions are ideal and the frog is actively foraging, it may be a brilliant leaf green. The flanks are blue barred with white or light yellow. The toes and fingers are orange. The belly is white. Red-eyes have large and well-developed toepads and are adept at both leaping and walking through their elevated homes. The irises (irides) are deep red and the pupils are vertically elliptical.

This frog is now available in xanthic (creamy yellow with yellow eyes) and albino (yellow with red eyes) morphs.

Red-eyed treefrogs are nocturnal. Males produce their nonmelodious

This red-eye is preparing to jump to a nearby perch.

(to all but females of the species), usually single-syllabled (but sometimes ratcheting) calls while sitting on pond edge vegetation.

Size and Lifespan

Adult at 2 to 2½ inches (5.1–6 cm), this very pretty treefrog may live for more than 10 years in captivity.

Natural Range

This treefrog, perhaps the most readily recognized treefrog in the world, ranges from southern Mexico through Panama. There is a possibility that it occurs in northern Colombia as well.

Captive Care

The caging for one or two red-eyes can be as simple or complex as you choose. A 10-gallon (37.8-L) tank with a damp paper towel on the bottom and containing a small potted philodendron or schleffera will suffice, but a properly planted terrarium with a small waterfall or pond is more aesthetically pleasing.

Red-eyes are quite at home with a relatively dry substrate and a small dish of clean water. Keep the cage clean. A lack of absolute cleanliness will most assuredly eventually transmit potentially lethal pathogens to your leaf frogs.

The blue lateral patterning can be variable.

Red-eyed treefrogs are nocturnal. They usually sleep soundly, scrunched down, eyes tightly closed, and feet drawn beneath them, by day. The frogs awaken and hunt at night. They can hop, but often walk slowly in a hand-over-hand manner. In most cases, a screen top that allows ventilation is more satisfactory than a glass top. Proper cage humidity should be maintained by misting the tank as necessary.

Tanks of 29- to 100-gallon (110- to 378.5-L) capacity lend themselves particularly well to naturalistic setups. Besides foliage plants, perches such as sterilized driftwood or gnarled manzanita (do not use cedar or any limbs treated with fungicides or insecticides) branch can be provided. Water can be provided in a shallow bowl. Keep both the water and the aquarium glass clean.

Crickets, waxworms, butterworms, and most other insects are all avidly eaten. For adult frogs, the insects should be dusted with vitamin D_3-calcium powder once every week or 10 days. The insects given to fast-growing young frogs should be dusted with D_3-calcium powder twice weekly.

Breeding

Red-eyed treefrogs have a specialized reproductive biology. While being amplexed by a male, a female deposits her egg clusters on a leaf overhanging standing water. The female red-eye will often fold the leaf over the clutch, thus preventing some desiccation. The egg masses are contained within a gelatinous outer coating. The tensile strength of the gelatin deteriorates over the incubation time and at, or shortly following, hatching, the tadpoles wriggle free and drop into the water where they continue their lives in what we will call a typical manner. If the egg mass has been placed where the tadpoles miss the water when they drop, and if they cannot reach the water after a very few energetic wriggles, the larvae succumb.

Greater breeding success can be had if several male red-eyes are maintained with a single female. The jostling and grappling of the males seems to induce greater fertility. In greenhouse settings, communal breeding involving a dozen or so males to several females can be very productive.

Red-eyed treefrogs usually breed following a period of semidormancy or dry season rest. Males vocalize in short, coarse, "chucking" notes to draw females to the sites. Male red-eyes clasp the females just behind the female's front legs. This is termed axillary amplexus. Rising temperatures, increasing photoperiod, and higher humidity (especially the passing of a rainy frontal system) stimulates breeding. Only the males vocalize. Most adult females are larger and heavier-bodied than adult males. Males develop nuptial excrescences on their thumbs when reproductively active, and males tend to sit in a more erect manner (forelimbs less flexed).

Clutches contain from 15 to about 60 eggs. One female can lay several clutches a season. Captive females often choose a spot several inches above the water on the aquarium glass for a deposition site. These clutches should be gently removed from the glass by slowly sliding a dampened single-edge razor blade beneath the cluster, keeping the blade tightly against the glass. The eggs should then be moved to another receptacle and placed on a plant's leaf a few inches above a bowl of suitably pure water. Keep the air surrounding the repositioned egg cluster humid by covering the receptacle with a sheet of plastic wrap or a pane of glass.

All water used must be free of chlorines and chloramines. The water temperature must be appropriate for the species involved. Normal room temperature (78–82°F [25.5–27.8°C]) is satisfactory for the incubation of the eggs of these tropical, lowland frogs.

Red-eyed treefrog tadpoles will eat large quantities of good-quality fish food, including koi, trout, and catfish chows. The time period from hatching to metamorphosis is nearly two months.

Be certain you have a ready and steady supply of tiny feed insects available before you do breed these (or any other) frogs. Due to rapid growth rate the metamorphs are especially prone to MBD (metabolic bone disease) at this stage of their lives. Feed them heavily and frequently, and dust all food items with a good-quality D_3/calcium mixture.

Other Frogs with Similar Needs

Other treefrogs and most toads and frogs would thrive if provided the regimen of care suggested for the red-eyed treefrog. Research the precise needs of each individual species.

Red-eyed treefrogs are remarkably beautiful.

Green Treefrog

Hyla cinerea

Description

This is one of the prettiest of the North American treefrogs. The dorsum is usually a bright green but may vary from brown to dark forest green. The belly is white. Typically, an enamel white lateral stripe narrowly edged both above and below by darker pigment is present. This may run from the snout to the groin, be foreshortened or, in some populations, even be entirely absent. Tiny golden orange spots may be present on the dorsum. The skin is smooth. Males have a huge vocal sac and the call is an oft-repeated nasal "quonk."

Albinos of this frog are now available in the pet trade. These are pretty in a pallid sort of way, and they often have vision problems.

Size and Lifespan

A length of 2¼ inches (3.7 cm) is commonly attained. Females are more robust than the males and lack the vocal sac. Green treefrogs may live for more than six years in captivity.

Natural Range

This frog ranges southward from the Delmarva Peninsula and south-

The green treefrog is a beautiful species native to the American southeast.

ern Illinois to the Florida Keys and the Lower Rio Grande Valley of Texas.

Captive Care

Green treefrogs are very easily kept, but are quite difficult to cycle for breeding. Unless they are frightened, these are quiet frogs that will remain for long periods—sometimes for days!—in one spot. In a terrarium, they may be tightly huddled into a vertical corner. By an outdoor pond this may be on a cattail leaf or on other pond-side vegetation. Because they are inactive, several green treefrogs can be maintained in a cage the size of a 10-gallon (37.8-L) aquarium, 10 × 12 × 20 inches (25 × 30 × 51 cm), but more spacious quarters are better. Green treefrogs not only thrive in greenhouse setups, but will often readily colonize a backyard fish pond.

Although green treefrogs are found in humid regions of the country, and in the vicinity of ponds as well, they are seldom seen actually in the water, except during the breeding season. They do best in a humid, but not wet, terrarium in which sturdy plants are growing upon which they can rest. Plants also provide visual barriers for these shy frogs.

Male green treefrogs have immense vocal sacs.

Green treefrogs feed readily upon all types of insects. Crickets, waxworms, and butterworms are all avidly eaten. For adult frogs, the insects should be dusted with vitamin D_3-calcium powder once every seven to ten days. Insects fed to

Albino green treefrogs are now available.

baby green treefrogs should be dusted with vitamin-mineral supplements twice weekly.

Breeding

When attempting to cycle green treefrogs for breeding, allow the natural rhythms of the seasons to set the pace. Induce dormancy (or semi-dormancy) by reducing temperature and humidity while maintaining a natural photoperiod during the winter months. After 75 to 90 days, again increase warmth and elevate humidity while still retaining a naturally lengthening photoperiod. "Spring showers" can be provided by using a recirculating pump and a spray head for a couple of hours a night. Any water used must be chloramine and chlorine-free. Winter's nighttime lows should be 55–65°F (12.7–18°C) and the humidity should be about 50 percent. The night lows of summer should be in the low to mid-70°Fs (21–24°C) and highs in the low to mid-80°Fs (26.8–29°C). Summer's humidity should be from 80 to 100 percent, depending to some degree on whether the cage's rain head is in operation. Your green treefrogs will eat less during their winter cooling. Once the summer's elevated photoperiod, temperature, and humidity are begun, the misting should prompt ovulation and spermatogenesis within a week or two.

Male green treefrogs may call while sitting on a leaf or while on the edge of the water receptacle. If the females respond and are amplexed, they may produce several hundred

Although most green treefrogs have a white lateral stripe, some lack this feature.

eggs in clusters of several dozen each.

The question of reproductive cycling is simplified if you live in an area where green treefrogs can be maintained outside year round and if you have a backyard pond. As mentioned earlier, green treefrogs are not at all reluctant to colonize a small pond, and when outdoors, Mother Nature, taking full advantage of all natural cues, does all of the cycling. Most fish will avidly eat small tadpoles, so if you have fish in the pond, scoop the green treefrog egg clusters or the tadpoles out and raise them in an aquarium.

Tadpoles will hatch in three to five days. The tadpole stage can last from 40 to 90 days. Tadpoles have big appetites and will eat good-quality fish food.

Within a few days after becoming froglets, the metamorphs will have developed an almost insatiable appetite. Feed them heavily and frequently, and dust all food items with a good-quality D_3/calcium mixture at least twice weekly.

Other Treefrogs with Similar Needs

The Neotropical clown treefrog, *Hyla leucophyllata*, is a small, colorful species that is often available in the pet trade. The gray treefrog, *Hyla versicolor* complex, and the barking treefrog, *Hyla gratiosa*, are both indigenous to the eastern and central United States.

Dwarf Underwater Frog

Hymenochirus curtipes

Description

These are tiny, flattened, rather rough-skinned frogs that are entirely aquatic throughout their lives. Females have slightly larger dermal tubercles than the males. The ground color is olive gray and there is a profusion of darker spots dorsally. Males have a tiny pocket of skin present at the axis of each forelimb. The head is small and not distinct from the neck. The snout is narrow but rounded. The eyes are situated laterally. The forelimbs are small and the fingers are partially webbed. The rear legs are powerfully developed and the toes are fully webbed. There are horny claws on the innermost three toes of each foot.

There are several other species, but all are almost impossible to differentiate.

Dwarf underwater frogs are more often available at aquarium shops than at reptile dealers.

The breeding calls, produced while the frog is submerged, are weak purring clicks that are easily overlooked.

Size and Lifespan

Adults are only 1 to 1½ inches (2.5–3.8 cm) in length. Although the

Alert and active, dwarf underwater frogs require tiny food materials.

sexes are about the same length, females are the heavier bodied. The lifespan of the underwater frog is three to five years.

Natural Range

These frogs are captive bred in large numbers in Asia and in smaller numbers in America. Wild-collected individuals are occasionally collected and imported by tropical fish distributors. This is a tropical West African frog. They are always aquatic, preferring still, shallow, heavily vegetated waters in ditches, ponds, puddles, and rice paddies.

Captive Care

Dwarf underwater frogs are so small that four or five can be maintained in a 5-gallon (18.9-L) aquarium. The water in which they are kept must be free of chlorine and chloramines. Very gentle filtration is suggested. A water temperature of from 75 to 82°F (23.9–27.8°C) is best. Temperatures much below 70°F (21.1°C) can be fatal for these tropical frogs. These little frogs are often purchased as a component for a community tropical fish setup, but they are timid and do not compete well with the fish for food. They fare much better if kept in a small colony by themselves. Although these shy

Dwarf underwater frogs are adult at only 1¼ inches (3 cm) in body length.

frogs can survive in a plain tank, they do best in a tank containing a profusion of rooted and floating plants. Artificial hiding areas, such as halved flower pots or commercially available caves, should also be provided. Lighting will be necessary to promote plant growth. A substrate of aquarium gravel or small river rock is suggested.

Despite their aquatic lifestyle, dwarf underwater frogs will quickly escape from an aquarium that is not very tightly covered. Take special pains to secure the areas around protruding heaters and filter lines.

Both live and frozen foods are accepted. Blackworms, bloodworms, and rinsed brine shrimp, as well as daphnia and cyclops are excellent foods. Tiny bits of pelleted food may be eaten but is most often ignored by these frogs.

Partial water changes should be performed weekly and it is best if a major water change (¾ths to ⅞ths of the volume) occurs monthly.

Breeding

If adult, warm, healthy, and well fed, these frogs will often spawn spontaneously and repeatedly. Each clutch will consist of from 35 to about 100 eggs. Freshening of the aquarium water (a partial half-change, for example) with a slight drop in temperature will also help cycle these caudatans. If you choose to raise any tadpoles, the adult frogs should be moved to another tank. Although the frogs will probably ignore the eggs, they will ravenously consume the hatching tadpoles. Three to five clutches, each about a week and a half apart, may be produced before the frogs rest for the season. Gravid females are very heavy bodied. Amplexus is inguinal, the male grasping the female around the waist. Typically,

Dwarf underwater frogs thrive in a clean, warm aquarium.

the eggs are expelled and fertilized about halfway through a somersault when the frogs are inverted near the surface of the water.

At 75 to 80°F (23.9–26.7°C) the eggs will hatch in five to seven days and the tadpoles will require the tiniest of live food; infusoria is a good choice. As the tadpoles grow, the size of their food can be increased. The tadpoles will metamorphose in about 4½ months.

Other Aquatic Frogs with Similar Needs

Several other frog species will thrive in the conditions discussed above. Among the hardiest and most readily available are the various clawed frogs (genus *Xenopus*) and Suriname toads (genus *Pipa*). However, these anurans are larger when adult and will require larger aquaria. The small rice paddy frog (also called the oriental floating frog), *Occidozyga lima*, is also usually available. Although very different from the several underwater frogs, the rice paddy frog will thrive in aquaria having ample floating plants. It will have to be fed with tiny crickets dropped onto the floating plants or with bits of worms presented on a broom straw or small forceps, but otherwise, conditions similar to those above are adequate.

Axolotl

Ambystoma mexicanum

Description

The axolotl (pronounced *axe-oh-low-til*) is one of the more spectacular of the few species of salamanders commonly encountered in the American pet trade. Because of its origin, this salamander is commonly (and appropriately) referred to as the Mexican axolotl.

This is an impressive salamander, with a heavy body, prominent costal grooves, bushy red or black external gills, and well-formed but lidless eyes. The legs are also well developed and used for walking along the bottom of its aquarium. When the salamander is swimming, the limbs are usually folded back against the body.

Originally of an olive brown to olive gray coloration, with dark eyes, axolotls are now available in several "designer" colors. These include albino (white with pink eyes), piebald (variously mottled with white and olive with dark eyes), leucistic (pure white with dark eyes), black (a totally descriptive name), and a beautiful gold (with either pink or dark eyes).

The axolotl is a neotenic salamander species. This means that it attains

Although metamorphosis is rare, this axolotl is a fully metamorphed, terrestrial adult.

sexual maturity while a larva, and that it normally retains its larval characteristics throughout its life. Rarely, an axolotl will spontaneously metamorphose (assume a terrestrial adult stage—resorb the gills and tail fin and develop a more complex skin, eyelids, and stronger legs), and the addition of certain hormones—iodine does not work!—can also induce metamorphosis. Terrestrial axolotls are usually far less robust than the aquatic larvae and often succumb within a few months of life on land.

Size and Lifespan

Hatchlings are about as big as a large comma (**,**) but eat ravenously and grow quite quickly. Adults attain an overall length of from 7 to 9 inches (17.8–22.5 cm) and are of robust appearance. If properly cared for, a lifespan of from 10 to more than 20 years is not uncommon.

Natural Range

The onetime range of the axolotl included several cool-water lakes located southeast of Mexico City. However, extensive habitat degradation has occurred, dramatically reducing axolotl populations. The actual status of the creature is unknown, but it seems likely that there is now a far greater number in

This is a juvenile albino axolotl.

captivity than in the onetime wilds of central Mexico.

Captive Care

Under normal conditions, this is a fully aquatic salamander that never assumes the adult stage of life. It is typified by a smooth skin, lidless eyes, a large tail fin, and three prominent, bushy gills on each side of the head.

Axolotls thrive best in cool water (56–72°F [13–22°C]). Excessively warm water may induce internal problems that cause the salamander to float and may allow the proliferation of skin diseases (such as fungus) as well.

When kept communally, axolotls can belie the reputation of benign coexistence that is often attributed to salamanders. Larger axolotls will readily eat their smaller siblings, breeders will eat the eggs they are

depositing, and hungry axolotls may bite off the legs, gills, or tail tips of tankmates. This is especially true during the feeding frenzies that almost invariably accompany the introduction of live food to the axolotl aquarium. These salamanders become so intent on feeding (chopped earthworms, black worms, or other such fare brings about these frenzies) that they then will bite anything they bump into. This behavior occurs at all ages. Although removed appendages—legs, tail tips, or gill stalks—are eventually regrown, it is, of course, better if the injury never occurs. Visual barriers will help reduce aggression.

While on the subject of food, acceptable foods for the salamanders vary somewhat with the axolotl's age and size. Hatchlings prefer live food such as chopped blackworms, brine shrimp, or daphnia. Hatchlings will seldom accept prepared foods. Although axolotls of all sizes relish fresh animal protein, as the salamanders grow they become a bit more adventuresome, and will sample sinking trout chow, catfish chow, and koi pellets. Once accustomed to prepared foods the axolotls will learn to swim to the surface and eat floating foods. The use of floating food allows the easy removal of any pellets that are not eaten within a reasonable time. The size of the pellets should be tailored to the size of the axolotls for which they are intended.

Axolotls acclimate to most aquarium conditions very readily. Water must be clean (this means ammonia-free), cool (cool water holds more dissolved oxygen), and well filtered. Water having a pH of about 7.2 is preferred. Chlorine or chloramines must be removed before introducing the salamander to the tank. Whether tiny hatchlings or 9-inch-long (23-cm) adults, the salamanders should be provided ample room. Although a dozen or more hatchlings can be kept in a 5-gallon (19.9-L) aquarium, a single adult will require a 10-gallon (37.8-L) (or preferably larger) aquarium. Several adults should have a water volume of not less than 50 gallons (189 L).

If you provide a substrate it must be of pebbles sufficiently large that your axolotls cannot ingest them. Keep in mind that food and debris quickly settle between large pebbles, and may make it difficult to stabilize your water quality. A tank with only a few smooth stones or even a bare bottom will be much easier to keep clean. Adding aquarium plants is fine but will require that you provide bright light, or the plants quickly die. Nonrooted plants such as hornwort are ideal. Any additional ornamentation should have smooth edges and no points to assure that a swimming axolotl does not accidentally injure itself. Axolotls do not seem to need a hiding area.

Breeding

Axolotls are one of the easiest salamanders to condition, cycle, and breed. Besides the physical condition of the salamanders themselves,

success will depend also upon water quality and temperature.

Female axolotls are of more robust build than the males, have a broader head and a shorter snout. When reproductively active, males have a noticeably swollen cloaca. It seems as if axolotls are stimulated to breed by the shortened photoperiod and cooler days of winter. The probability of successful breeding will be enhanced if you lower the water level by about 50 percent for a week or two and then refill the tank with fresh (dechlorinated/ dechloramined) water that is slightly cooler than the tank water. Females in breeding readiness will push the males about with their snout (probably in response to emitted pheromones). Males will deposit a spermatophore on the bottom of the tank. The sperm-bearing cap is picked up by the female with her cloacal labia. Eggs are then deposited singly on plants, aquarium decorations, or on the sides and bottom of the aquarium. Either the eggs or the adults should be removed soon after laying is finished, or the eggs may be eaten by the breeders.

Eggs seem best maintained at a water temperature of about 60°F (15.5°C) and should be gently aerated. Hatching occurs in 12 to 24 days. Babies will usually eat live baby brine shrimp (washed in fresh water) or finely chopped blackworms the day after hatching. Thickets of hornwort (or similar water plants) will provide visual barriers and help prevent aggression and cannibalism.

Japanese Fire-bellied Newt
Cynops pyrrhogaster

Description

This is one of the prettiest of the larger newts, but it is not always readily available. The color is simple but striking. This newt is a rich brown dorsally and a bright red, with or without darker vermiculations, ventrally. Well-defined parotoid glands are present and the glandular secretions are quite toxic. During the breeding season the tail of the male takes on a bluish cast and a tail tip filament develops. The head is well defined, broad, flattened, and angular.

Size and Lifespan

This is a robust 5-inch (12.7-cm) long species. A lifespan of well over 20 years is possible.

Natural Range

The Japanese fire-bellied newt is aptly named. It is not only flame bellied but is restricted in distribution to Japan. It can be found in quiet ponds, swamps, and slow-moving streams.

Captive Care

Despite being most often encountered by hobbyists in the aquaria of

The Japanese fire-bellied newt is a large and hardy species.

tropical fish stores, the Japanese fire-belly is not a warm-water newt. Water temperatures in the 60°Fs (15–20.5°C) and low 70°Fs (21–23.9°C) are preferred. The water must be free of chlorine and chloramines. This newt may be maintained under aquatic conditions throughout the year or it may be offered terrestrial conditions when it is not breeding. If aquatic, the aquarium should be well stocked with living plants. Juveniles are more terrestrially inclined than the adults and will do well in a woodland or semiaquatic terrarium. If a semi-aquatic setup is used, easy access to and from the water is mandatory.

Newts are predatory creatures and feed on all types of small worms, insects, and arthropods. Aquatic newts also eat the eggs of fish, frogs, and other salamanders, as well as their own eggs.

From one to several fire-bellied newts may be kept in a 10-gallon (37.8-L) aquarium. This enclosure may be set up as a gently filtered, fully aquatic aquarium, as a semi-aquatic terrarium, or, if your newts are not in breeding condition, as a woodland terrarium.

In all cases the temperatures should be below 75°F (23.9°C).

Japanese fire-bellied newts attain an adult size of about 5 inches (12.5 cm).

Breeding

This newt cycles most readily for breeding if cooled to 48 to 55°F (8.9–12.8°C) for two to three months during the short days of winter; however, some have been bred with no cooling period having been provided. Freshening of the aquarium water (a partial half-change, for example) with a slight drop in temperature will also help cycle these caudatans.

Fire-bellied newts will continue feeding while cooled but will do so rather sparingly. Do not overfeed or you will sour the aquarium water. Begin feeding your newts more heavily as their waters are warmed to summer temperatures.

Provide a natural photoperiod year round. The warming water and lengthening days of spring will stimulate your newts to begin their courtship activities.

The courtship of the fire-bellied newt is intriguingly complex.

Pheromones (stimulatory scents) are produced in the male's chin glands. During amplexus the male newt will swim around or position himself in front of the female. He may butt her with his head or rub her with his chin, bringing these stimulants into play. Elaborate body positioning and tail fanning will be seen to help disperse the pheromones. During courtship the male produces a spermatophore, the sperm-bearing cap of which is picked up by the female with her cloaca. After accepting the sperm packet, the female lays her eggs singly (or in very small clusters) among floating plants or on the leaves of rooted plants. The female positions the adhesive eggs with her hind feet.

Since newts will avidly eat their own eggs, the eggs and adults should be separated after deposition is completed.

Eggs hatch in 15 to 40 days, depending on water temperature. Newly hatched newt larvae are tiny

This adult Japanese fire-bellied newt is at home in a 125-gallon filtered aquarium.

and after absorbing the yolk sac (usually several days after hatching), will require the tiniest of food items. Most prefer live prey, accepting daphnia, cyclops, and other pond fare, as well as chopped black and/or tubifex worms. Offer only as much as the baby newts can eat, for if left, the excess will pollute the aquarium water. As the larval newts grow, so, too, may the size of the offered food items be increased. At about ½ inch (1.2 cm) in length, these creatures are well able to eat whole tubbier and black worms. If brine shrimp is given it should be washed free of its salt content.

Fire-bellied newts often take from four and a half to six months to metamorphose. As metamorphosis nears, the water level in the aquarium should be lowered and a heavy cover of floating plants (or small pieces of corkbark) should be pro-

vided. The larvae will usually clamber about on the surface plants or near the water surface on the cork while resorting their gills and undergoing skin structure and other anatomical changes. Once metamorphosis is completed, the juveniles will usually do best in a damp woodland terrarium. If fed amply, the baby newts will grow rapidly.

Other Newts with Similar Needs

Spanish marbled newts, *Triturus marmoratus*, crested newts, *Triturus cristatus* complex, and Hong Kong warty newts, *Paramesotriton hongkongensis*, have needs similar to the Japanese fire-bellied newt. All are cool water species and are capable of thriving in an aquatic setting or of being terrestrial other than in the breeding season. All are very long lived.

143

Eastern Newts

Notophthalmus viridescens

Description

It is the aquatic adults of the several subspecies of the red-spotted newt of eastern North America that are most often available to American hobbyists. The adults are 4 to 5 inches (10–12.7 cm) in length. The nominate form, the red-spotted newt, *Notophthalmus v. viridescens*, usually bears a row of well–defined, black-edged, red spots on each side of its back. On *N. v. dorsalis*, the broken-striped newt, the red spots are extended into black edged stripes that are usually broken, but that may be almost complete. The central newt, *N. v. louisianensis*, may either have or lack the red spots, but if present they are poorly defined. The peninsula newt, *N. v. piaropicola*, is of very dark dorsal coloration and lacks the red dorsal spots.

Occasionally, efts, the land stage of these newts, are available. These are geographically and ontogenetically variable in color. Young efts from the cool, humid Northeast southward into the Appalachian Mountains are usually a spectacular red-orange with black-edged red dorsolateral spots. Older efts, and

The red eft is the terrestrial stage in the life of the red-spotted newt.

efts of all ages from other, less hospitable areas may be of dingier ground color.

Reproductively active males have a high tail fin and thickened rear legs bearing black, horny excrescences on their inner surfaces. Their toetips are also black.

Size and Lifespan

As efts, these newts are seldom more than 3 inches (7.6 cm) in total length. Adults may attain a length of about 5 inches (12.7 cm).

Like most newts, if well cared for, the eastern newts have a long lifespan. Wild-collected adults have lived for more than 20 years as captives.

Natural Range

Collectively, the subspecies of this newt range southward from southern Quebec and Ontario to southern Florida and southeastern Texas.

• The red-spotted newt ranges southward from Quebec to central Georgia.

• The range of the central newt covers a vast area from southern Ontario to southeastern Texas and eastward to northern Florida and central South Carolina.

• The broken-striped newt occurs only in southeastern North Carolina and northwestern South Carolina.

The aquatic adult red-spotted newt is hued in shades of olive accented by small, black-rimmed red dorsolateral spots.

• The peninsula newt is restricted in range to the southern four-fifths of the Florida Peninsula.

Captive Care

The eastern newts have a complex life history. Under ideal climatic conditions, these newts begin life as an egg, then sequentially are aquatic larvae, terrestrial efts, then aquatic adults. Eggs, larvae, and adults are cryptically colored; the efts, instinctively relying on acrid glandular secretions to avoid predation, can be spectacularly bright and obvious.

These salamanders are extremely cold-tolerant. They are easily able to withstand water temperatures in the 40°Fs (4.4–9.4°C), and prefer that highs not exceed the mid-70°Fs (23.9°C).

An unheated 10-gallon (37.8-L) terrarium will easily house several efts. Several adults will thrive in an aquarium of the same size, also unheated.

Breeding

The eastern newts are all easily maintained and can be bred in captivity with little more than minimal cycling. They should be cooled throughout the winter, but do not need to be hibernated. Water temperatures of 45–65°F (7.2–18°C) will suffice. Maintain a natural photoperiod. As the days grow longer in the spring, allow the water temperature to warm somewhat. Males should soon develop visible secondary characteristics such as a large tail fin and the horny excrescences on the rear limbs.

The copulatory embrace of the newt is called amplexus. Males deposit spermatophores. After they have been stimulated by courtship, the females pick up the sperm packets in their cloacal lips and fertilization of the eggs is internal. As the adhesive eggs are laid, the female manipulates them into place on sticks or the leaves of vegetation

Although still in their terrestrial stage, these broken-striped newts are almost ready to resume life in the water.

with her hind feet. She may lay more than 300 eggs. The incubation duration varies according to temperature, being somewhat less than three weeks if the temperature is warm to more than six weeks if water temperature is cool.

Newt larvae are nourished by the yolk sac for several days following hatching. When they do begin feeding they require the tiniest of food items. Most prefer live prey, accepting daphnia, cyclops, and other pond fare, as well as chopped black and/or tubifex worms. Offer only as much as the baby newts can eat, for the excess will spoil and pollute your water. As the larval newts grow, so too may the size of the offered food items be increased.

Metamorphosis can occur in as little as three months, but more often takes from four and a half to six months. The time of their transformation from larval to adult structure can be fraught with difficulties for newts. Besides changing epidermal structure, they are then changing from external gills to functional lungs. It is at this time that drowning is most possible. To forestall that possibility, it is best to reduce the depth of the water in which the newts are living, and to provide a denser cover of surface plants into which the babies can crawl. Once metamorphosis is completed the juveniles should be removed to suitable quarters. From that point on, providing they are amply provisioned, most newts will grow rapidly.

Other Newts with Similar Needs

Oriental fire-bellied newts, *Cynops orientalis*, and Pygmy marbled newts, *Triturus pygmaeus*, will thrive under the conditions delineated above. The adults of these species are aquatic during the late winter to early summer breeding season, but usually assume a terrestrial existence at other times. All require cool terrarium temperatures.

Glossary

Albino: Lacking black pigment.

Ambient temperature: The temperature of the surrounding environment.

Amplexus: The breeding embrace of amphibians.

Anal plate: The large scute immediately anterior to the cloaca on snakes and some lizards.

Anerythristic: Lacking red pigment.

Anterior: Toward the front.

Anuran: A tailless amphibian; frogs, toads, and treefrogs.

Anus: The external opening of the cloaca; the vent.

Brille: The transparent "spectacle" covering the eyes of a snake.

Brumation: Often used to describe reptilian and amphibian hibernation.

Caudal: Pertaining to the tail.

Caudatan: A tailed amphibian; a salamander or newt.

cb/cb: Captive bred, captive born.

Chelonian: A turtle or tortoise.

Cloaca: The common chamber into which digestive, urinary, and reproductive systems empty and that itself opens exteriorly through the vent.

Constricting: Wrapping tightly in coils and squeezing.

Crepuscular: Active at dusk and/or dawn.

Diapause: A temporary (and normal) cessation in the embryonic development.

Deposition site: The spot chosen by the female to have young.

Dorsal: Pertaining to the back; upper surface.

Dorsolateral: Pertaining to the upper sides.

Dorsum: The upper surface.

Ectothermic: "Cold-blooded."

Egg mass: The gelatinous covered egg cluster deposited by many amphibians.

Endothermic: "Warm-blooded."

Erythristic: A prevalence of red pigment.

Form: An identifiable species or subspecies.

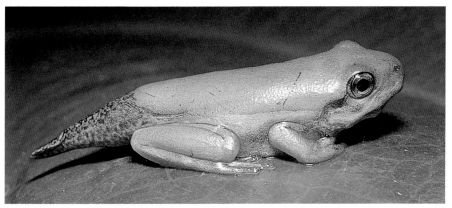

Most frogs have a tail for a few hours or days after metamorphosing from the tadpole stage.

Genus: A taxonomic classification of a group of species having similar characteristics. The genus falls between the next higher designation of "family" and the next lower designation of "species." Genera is the plural of genus. The generic name is always capitalized when written.

Glottis: The opening of the windpipe.

Gravid: Describing the reptilian equivalent of mammalian pregnancy.

Hemipenes: The dual copulatory organs of male lizards and snakes.

Hemipenis: The singular form of hemipenes.

Herpetoculture: The captive breeding of reptiles and amphibians.

Herpetoculturist: One who indulges in herpetoculture.

Herps: A stylized term referring to all reptiles and amphibians.

Herpetology: The study (often scientifically oriented) of reptiles and amphibians.

Hybrid: Offspring resulting from the interbreeding of two species or non-contiguous subspecies.

Infusoria: A heterogenous mixture of tiny plant and animal species that often occur in decaying plant matter.

Intergrade: Offspring resulting from the breeding of two contiguous subspecies.

Jacobson's organs: Highly enervated olfactory pits in the palate of snakes and lizards.

Juvenile: A young or immature specimen.

Labial: Pertaining to the lips.

Labial pit(s): Heat-sensory depressions on the lips of some boas.

Lateral: Pertaining to the side.

A normal striped California kingsnake.

Melanism: A profusion of black pigment.

Mental: The scale at the tip of the lower lip.

Metachrosis: Color changes.

Middorsal: Pertaining to the middle of the back.

Midventral: Pertaining to the center of the belly or abdomen.

Neonate: A newborn baby of a live-bearing species.

Nocturnal: Active at night.

Ocular stripe: A stripe on the side of the head that passes through the eye.

Ontogenetic: Age-related (color) changes.

Photoperiod: The daily/seasonally variable length of the hours of daylight.

Postocular: To the rear of the eye.

Race: A subspecies.

Rostral: The (often modified) scale on the tip of the snout.

Scute: A large scale.

Species: A group of similar creatures that produce viable young when breeding. The taxonomic designation that falls beneath genus and above subspecies. Abbreviation, "sp."

Squamata: The composite grouping of lizards and snakes.

Subcaudal: Beneath the tail.

Subspecies: The subdivision of a species. A race that may differ slightly in color, size, scalation, or other criteria. Abbreviation, "ssp."

Taxonomy: The science of classification of plants and animals.

Terrestrial: Land-dwelling.

Thermoregulate: To regulate (body) temperature by choosing a warmer or cooler environment.

Tympanum: The external eardrum of anurans.

Vent: The external opening of the cloaca; the anus.

Venter: The underside of a creature; the belly.

Ventral: Pertaining to the undersurface or belly.

Ventrolateral: Pertaining to the sides of the venter (=belly).

Resources

Herpetological Societies

Reptile and amphibian support groups exist in the form of clubs, monthly magazines, and professional societies, in addition to the herp expos, and other commercial functions mentioned elsewhere.

Herpetological societies (or clubs) exist in major cities in North America, Europe, and other areas of the world. Most have monthly meetings, some publish newsletters, and many host or sponsor field trips, picnics, or indulge in various other interactive functions. Among the members are enthusiasts of varying expertise. Information about these clubs can often be learned by querying pet shop employees, high school science teachers, university biology department professors, or curators or employees at the department of herpetology at local museums and zoos. All such clubs welcome inquiries and new members.

Two of the professional herpetological societies are

Society for the Study of Amphibians
    and Reptiles (SSAR)
Department of Zoology
Miami University
Oxford, OH 45056

Herpetologist's League
c/o Texas National Heritage
    Program
Texas Parks and Wildlife
    Department
4200 Smith School Road
Austin, TX 78744

The SSAR publishes two quarterly journals: *Herpetological Review* contains husbandry, range extensions, news on ongoing field studies, etc., while the *Journal of Herpetology* contains articles more oriented toward academic herpetology.

Reptiles Magazine publishes articles on all aspects of herpetology and herpetoculture. This monthly also carries classified ads and news about herp expos. Contact this publication at *Reptiles*, P.O. Box 6050, Mission Viejo, CA 92690.

One of the most important Internet addresses is *www.kingsnake.com*. This site provides up-to-date news on expos and herp clubs, an immensely active classified section that offers both amphibians and reptiles, interactive moderated forums, periodic chats, and Web radio interviews. Because of the ability to post and view photos of the species being offered for sale, this site

Tangerine Honduran milks are eagerly sought by hobbyists.

A portrait of an oriental fire-bellied toad.

should be of great interest to all hobbyists.

Also see *www.faunaclassifieds .com*. This is another important Web address.

Caudata.org is an excellent Web site that pertains exclusively to newts and salamanders.

Books

Bartlett, Patricia P., Billy Griswold, and R. D. Bartlett. *Reptiles, Amphibians, and Invertebrates*. Hauppauge, NY: Barron's Educational Series, Inc., 2001.

Bartlett, R. D. and Patricia Bartlett. *Designer Reptiles and Amphibians*. Hauppauge, NY: Barron's Educational Series, Inc., 2002.

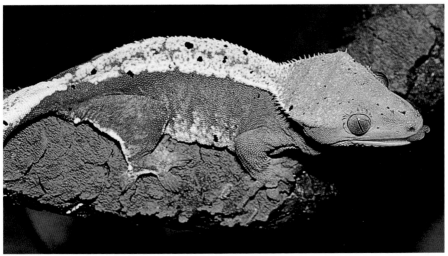

Crested geckos are not colorful, yet they are attractive.

Bartlett, R. D. *Frogs, Toads, and Treefrogs*. Hauppauge, NY: Barron's Educational Series, Inc., 1996.

Bartlett, R. D. and Patricia Bartlett. *Terrarium and Cage Construction and Care*. Hauppauge, NY: Barron's Educational Series, Inc., 1999.

This is a neonate northern blue-tongued skink, Tiliqua scincoides intermedia.

Index

Page numbers in boldface type indicate photographs.

154

Yellow red–eyed treefrogs have now been developed by herpetoculturists. These are red-eyed in name only.